# Drush for Developers

*Second Edition*

Effectively manage Drupal projects using Drush

**Juampy Novillo Requena**

BIRMINGHAM - MUMBAI

# Drush for Developers
## *Second Edition*

First published: April 2012

Second edition: January 2015

Production reference: 1240115

Published by Packt Publishing Ltd.
Livery Place
35 Livery Street
Birmingham B3 2PB, UK.

ISBN 978-1-78439-378-6

www.packtpub.com

# Credits

**Author**
Juampy Novillo Requena

**Reviewers**
Greg Anderson
Chris Burgess
Jonathan Araña Cruz
Jeremy French
Todd Zebert

**Commissioning Editor**
Dipika Gaonkar

**Acquisition Editor**
Meeta Rajani

**Content Development Editor**
Anila Vincent

**Technical Editor**
Arvind Koul

**Copy Editor**
Relin Hedly

**Project Coordinator**
Neha Bhatnagar

**Proofreaders**
Bridget Braund
Ameesha Green

**Indexer**
Tejal Soni

**Production Coordinator**
Alwin Roy

**Cover Work**
Alwin Roy

# About the Author

**Juampy Novillo Requena** started working as a web developer in London. After spending a few years developing with plain PHP, Symfony, and Ruby on Rails, he discovered Drupal. Drawn by the Drupal community and the *mind-blowing effect of getting a project done 10 times faster than before*, Juampy has never looked back.

Since then, he's become more and more involved in the issue queues, which in turn led him to become a maintainer of core and contributed modules. He organizes events, gives sessions at national and international conferences, and has written the book *Drush User's Guide, Packt Publishing*. He feels privileged to experiment, have fun, and be challenged every day. He is known as `juampy` on `Drupal.org` and IRC. His Twitter account is `@juampy72`.

This book is the result of my two years working at Lullabot. Most of the contents explained here were originated by discussions or contributions within the team. I am very thankful to the team who worked on the MSNBC project, where we collaboratively developed and implemented best practices that are represented in this book.

I also want to thank the technical reviewers; their suggestions and corrections leveraged this book to a higher level.

Finally, a personal acknowledgement to the city of Niamey, Niger, where I did most of the writing.

# About the Reviewers

**Greg Anderson** is an open source contributions engineer working on Drupal and WordPress at Pantheon in San Francisco. He has been contributing to Drush since just before the release of version 2, and remains an active co-maintainer to this day.

**Chris Burgess** is currently making the world better by building open source tools for activist and nonprofit organizations to campaign and communicate. He has been developing with Drupal since 2006, and he is immensely grateful to the Drupal and wider open source communities for the learning and sharing environment that they foster. Chris is based in Dunedin, New Zealand, with his two sons, Hunter and Rowan, and partner, Saira. He works for Fuzion Aotearoa, and you can reach him at `@xurizaemon` on Twitter, `xur1z` on IRC, or his `Drupal.org` profile at `https://www.drupal.org/u/xurizaemon`.

**Jonathan Araña Cruz** is a co-maintainer of Drush. He combines both sysadmin and Drupal development work. Jonathan has contributed several modules to Drupal, and as a sysadmin, he manages Infrastructure as Code with Puppet.

Jonathan's Drupal profile can be found at `https://www.drupal.org/u/jonhattan`.

**Jeremy French** has worked in web development for over a decade, floating through a wasteland of bespoke Content Management Systems, before finding Drupal. He has developed sites for a number of household names and blue chips, as well as a few interesting start-ups. Currently, he is working for a small agency, living the dream of distributed working.

**Todd Zebert** has been involved with Drupal since early version 6. He creates websites and web apps with a variety of technologies. Currently, Todd works as a lead web developer for Miles.

Todd has a diverse background in technology, including infrastructure, network engineering, project management, and IT leadership. His experience with web development started with the original Mosaic graphical web browser, SHTML/CGI, and Perl. His fondness for Drupal and his interest in workflow, efficiency, repeatable best practices, and DevOps drives his interest in Drush.

Todd is an entrepreneur involved with the start-up community. He's a believer in volunteering, open source, and contributing back. He's an advocate for Science, Technology, Engineering, Art, and Math (STEAM) education.

I'd like to thank the Drupal community, which is like no other.

Finally, I'd like to thank my pre-teen son with whom I get to share my interest in technology and program video games together.

# www.PacktPub.com

## Support files, eBooks, discount offers, and more

For support files and downloads related to your book, please visit www.PacktPub.com.

Did you know that Packt offers eBook versions of every book published, with PDF and ePub files available? You can upgrade to the eBook version at www.PacktPub.com and as a print book customer, you are entitled to a discount on the eBook copy. Get in touch with us at service@packtpub.com for more details.

At www.PacktPub.com, you can also read a collection of free technical articles, sign up for a range of free newsletters and receive exclusive discounts and offers on Packt books and eBooks.

https://www2.packtpub.com/books/subscription/packtlib

Do you need instant solutions to your IT questions? PacktLib is Packt's online digital book library. Here, you can search, access, and read Packt's entire library of books.

## Why subscribe?

- Fully searchable across every book published by Packt
- Copy and paste, print, and bookmark content
- On demand and accessible via a web browser

## Free access for Packt account holders

If you have an account with Packt at www.PacktPub.com, you can use this to access PacktLib today and view 9 entirely free books. Simply use your login credentials for immediate access.

.

# Table of Contents

# Preface

In this book, I share with you how I use Drush in my day-to-day work. When working on Drupal projects, Drush is omnipresent. It is a key tool to debug code, run small scripts, and discover APIs. However, this is just the beginning; Drush's real potential comes when teams use it to define a development workflow.

## What this book covers

*Chapter 1, Introduction, Installation, and Basic Usage*, begins with Drush's requirements and installation and then shows its basic usage through examples.

*Chapter 2, Keeping Database Configuration and Code Together*, explains how to export configuration from the database into code in order to share it with the rest of the team and other environments.

*Chapter 3, Running and Monitoring Tasks in Drupal Projects*, gives different options to run tasks in Drupal projects such as cron, Batch API, and custom scripts.

*Chapter 4, Error Handling and Debugging*, explores tools that help us catch and process errors, so as to navigate through the available hooks and functions in our project.

*Chapter 5, Managing Local and Remote Environments*, unveils all the magic behind site aliases using a typical Drupal project that involves production and development environments.

*Chapter 6, Setting Up a Development Workflow*, leverages all the concepts covered in the book by defining a development workflow for a team.

# What you need for this book

Here are the system requirements to run the examples in the book:

- Operating system: Any Unix-based system such as:
    - Ubuntu (any version), available at http://www.ubuntu.com
    - MAC OS X (any version)
- Software:
    - PHP 5.2 or higher, available at http://www.php.net
    - MySQL 5.0 or higher, available at http://www.mysql.com
    - Apache 2.0 or higher, available at http://www.apache.org
    - Drupal 7, available at http://drupal.org
    - Git, available at http://git-scm.com
    - Jenkins, available at https://wiki.jenkins-ci.org

# Who this book is for

This book will fit best to backend developers with a basic knowledge of Drupal's APIs and some experience using the command line. Perhaps, you already worked on one or two Drupal projects, but have never dived deep into Drush's toolset. In any case, this book will give you a lot of advice by covering real-world challenges in Drupal projects that can be solved using Drush.

# Conventions

In this book, you will find a number of styles of text that distinguish between different kinds of information. Here are some examples of these styles and an explanation of their meaning.

Code words in text, database table names, folder names, filenames, file extensions, pathnames, dummy URLs, user input, and Twitter handles are shown as follows: "Drush runs using a different PHP.ini configuration than the web server that does not have a request timeout."

A block of code is set as follows:

```
/**
 * Callback to delete revisions using Batch API.
 */
function node_revision_delete_batch_process($content_type,
  $max_revisions, &$context) {
  if (!isset($context['sandbox']['nids'])) {
    // Set initial values.
    $context['sandbox']['nids'] = node_revision_delete_candidates
      ($content_type, $max_revisions);
    $context['sandbox']['current'] = 0;
    $context['sandbox']['total'] = count($context
      ['sandbox']['nids']);
  }
}
```

When we wish to draw your attention to a particular part of a code block, the relevant lines or items are set in bold:

```
/**
 * Callback to delete revisions using Batch API.
 */
function node_revision_delete_batch_process($content_type,
  $max_revisions, &$context) {
  if (!isset($context['sandbox']['nids'])) {
    // Set initial values.
    $context['sandbox']['nids'] = node_revision_delete_
      candidates($content_type, $max_revisions);
    $context['sandbox']['current'] = 0;
    $context['sandbox']['total'] =
      count($context['sandbox']['nids']);
  }
}
```

Any command-line input or output is written as follows:

```
$ drush php-script logging.php
success: marks a successful message.          [success]
error: reports an error message.              [error]
warning: is used to alert about something.    [warning]
```

**New terms** and **important words** are shown in bold. Words that you see on the screen, for example, in menus or dialog boxes for example, appear in the text like this: "You can test it by clicking on the **Build Now** link on the left navigation menu and then inspecting the Jenkins console output."

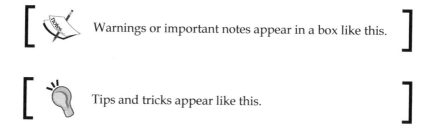

Warnings or important notes appear in a box like this.

Tips and tricks appear like this.

# Reader feedback

Feedback from our readers is always welcome. Let us know what you think about this book—what you liked or disliked. Reader feedback is important for us as it helps us develop titles that you really get the most out of.

To send us general feedback, simply e-mail to feedback@packtpub.com, and mention the book's title in the subject of your message.

If there is a topic that you have expertise in and you are interested in either writing or contributing to a book, see our author guide at www.packtpub.com/authors.

# Customer support

Now that you are the proud owner of a Packt book, we have a number of things to help you to get the most from your purchase.

# Downloading the example code

You can download the example code files from your account at http://www.packtpub.com for all the Packt Publishing books you have purchased. If you purchased this book elsewhere, you can visit http://www.packtpub.com/support and register to have the files e-mailed directly to you.

# Errata

Although we have taken every care to ensure the accuracy of our content, mistakes do happen. If you find a mistake in one of our books—maybe a mistake in the text or the code—we would be grateful if you could report this to us. By doing so, you can save other readers from frustration and help us improve subsequent versions of this book. If you find any errata, please report them by visiting http://www.packtpub. com/submit-errata, selecting your book, clicking on the **Errata Submission Form** link, and entering the details of your errata. Once your errata are verified, your submission will be accepted and the errata will be uploaded to our website or added to any list of existing errata under the Errata section of that title.

To view the previously submitted errata, go to https://www.packtpub.com/books/ content/support and enter the name of the book in the search field. The required information will appear under the **Errata** section.

# Piracy

Piracy of copyrighted material on the Internet is an ongoing problem across all media. At Packt, we take the protection of our copyright and licenses very seriously. If you come across any illegal copies of our works in any form on the Internet, please provide us with the location address or website name immediately so that we can pursue a remedy.

Please contact us at copyright@packtpub.com with a link to the suspected pirated material.

We appreciate your help in protecting our authors, and our ability to bring you valuable content.

# Questions

If you have a problem with any aspect of this book, you can contact us at questions@packtpub.com, and we will do our best to address the problem..

# 1
# Introduction, Installation, and Basic Usage

Drush is a command-line interface for Drupal. It can also serve as an alternative to write scripts using PHP instead of BASH. The Drush ecosystem is vast. Every year, at DrupalCon, the Drush core team gives an update on the bleeding edge features being developed by them and by contributors all over the world.

Tasks such as clearing caches, running database updates, executing batch scripts, and managing remote websites are just a glimpse of what you can do with Drush.

Here is an example. Imagine that you have pushed new code for your website and need to run database updates. Normally this would involve the following steps:

1. Back up your database.
2. Open your web browser and navigate to `http://example.com/user`.
3. Authenticate as administrator.
4. Navigate to `http://example.com/update.php`.
5. Run database updates and wait for a confirmation message.

Now, here is how you can accomplish the preceding steps with Drush:

```
$ drush @example.prod sql-dump > dump.sql
$ drush @example.prod updatedb --yes
```

That's it. We did not even have to open an SSH connection or a web browser. The first command created a database backup and the second one executed pending database updates. In both these commands, we used `@example.prod`, which is a Drush site alias used to load configuration details about a particular site. We will see Drush site aliases in detail in *Chapter 5, Managing Local and Remote Environments*.

Drush is highly customizable. You can adjust it to fit a specific workflow. This is especially helpful when working on a Drupal project within a team; you can define security policies, wrap commands with sensible defaults, sanitize a copy of the production database automatically, and so on. This is the area that this book will focus on. We will go through some common processes during a Drupal project and discover how we can automate or simplify them using Drush. Let's start!

This chapter is an introduction and will cover the following topics to get you up to speed:

- Installation requirements
- Drush command structure
- Understanding Drush's context system

# Installation requirements

The following are the installation requirements for Drush. If you have already installed it, simply make sure that you are running version 7.0.0-alpha5 (`https://github.com/drush-ops/drush/releases/tag/7.0.0-alpha5`) or higher by executing `drush --version` in the command line, and skip forward to the next section of this chapter.

# Operating system

Drush works on Unix-like operating systems (such as Ubuntu and OSX) and Windows operating systems.

If you use Windows, consider using something like VirtualBox (`https://www.virtualbox.org`) to install a virtual machine that runs, for example, Ubuntu (`http://www.ubuntu.com`). If you still want to use Drush on Windows, there is an installer available at `http://www.drush.org/drush_windows_installer`. Note, however, that the installer installs an older version of Drush, so some of the contents of this book won't work.

# PHP

Let's start by making sure that you have PHP 5.3.0 or greater installed. To do so, open a terminal and run the following command:

```
$ php -v
```

The output should look something like the following code screenshot:

```
PHP 5.5.9-1ubuntu4.3 (cli) (built: Jul  7 2014 16:36:58)
Copyright (c) 1997-2014 The PHP Group
Zend Engine v2.5.0, Copyright (c) 1998-2014 Zend Technologies
    with Zend OPcache v7.0.3, Copyright (c) 1999-2014, by Zend Technologies
    with Xdebug v2.2.3, Copyright (c) 2002-2013, by Derick Rethans
```

As you can see, I am using PHP 5.5.9. If you get a `Command not found` message or your version is lower than 5.3.0, you will need to install or upgrade PHP. Refer to your vendor documentation to do this as the steps will vary.

# Installing Composer

On Linux and OSX platforms, the recommended way to install Drush is through Composer (`https://getcomposer.org`), a dependency manager that has become the standard in the PHP world. Installing Composer can be accomplished with the following commands:

```
$ cd $HOME
$ curl -sS https://getcomposer.org/installer | php
$ sudo mv composer.phar /usr/local/bin/composer
```

If you find any issues while running the preceding commands or while installing it through a packaging system such as homebrew, then take a look at the official installation instructions for Composer (https://getcomposer.org/doc/00-intro. md#globally-on-osx-via-homebrew). Once you have completed the installation, you can verify that it works by running the following command:

```
$ composer about

Composer - Package Management for PHP

Composer is a dependency manager tracking local dependencies of your
projects and libraries.

See http://getcomposer.org/ for more information.
```

 If you have already installed Composer, make sure that it is up to date by running composer self-update (https://getcomposer. org/doc/03-cli.md#self-update).

# Drush installation on Linux and OSX

At the time of writing this book, the latest available version of Drush is 7.0.0-alpha5 (https://github.com/drush-ops/drush/releases/tag/7.0.0-alpha5). This is the version that we will use. The Drush core team does a fantastic job of keeping backwards compatibility between major versions, so if you have already installed a more recent version of Drush, you should be okay as practically all the examples in the book will work.

Let's go ahead and install Drush. Once Composer has been installed (see the previous section on installing Composer), you can install Drush with the following command:

```
$ composer global require drush/drush:7.0.0-alpha5 -v

Changed current directory to /home/juampy/.composer

./composer.json has been updated

Loading composer repositories with package information

Updating dependencies (including require-dev)

    - Installing drush/drush (7.0.0-alpha5)

    Downloading: 100%

    Extracting archive

drush/drush suggests installing youngj/httpserver

Writing lock file

Generating autoload files
```

The preceding command has downloaded Drush 7.0.0-alpha5 into $HOME/. composer/vendor/bin/drush. In order to use Drush from anywhere in the system, we need to make sure that Composer's bin directory is present at our $PATH environment variable. We can do so with the following commands:

```
$ sed -i '1i export PATH="$HOME/.composer/vendor/bin:$PATH"' \
    $HOME/.bashrc
$ source $HOME/.bashrc
```

Note the use of $HOME and $PATH, which are environment variables. $HOME contains the location of your home directory, while $PATH represents a list of directories to look for executable files. You can view the contents of these variables by executing echo $HOME or echo $PATH. Take a look at your home directory to check whether there is .bash_profile, .bash_login, or .profile file at $HOME. If you find them, adjust the preceding commands, so the $PATH variable is adjusted in these files as well.

Finally, we can test that Drush has been installed successfully and contains the right version:

```
$ cd $HOME
$ drush --version
 Drush Version   :  7.0.0-alpha5
```

# Manual installation

If you prefer to install Drush manually, then follow these steps:

1. Start by opening a web browser, and download and uncompress the contents of Drush 7.0.0-alpha5 (https://github.com/drush-ops/drush/releases/tag/7.0.0-alpha5) into your home directory.

2. Open a terminal and move the drush directory into your system's shared directory:

   ```
   $ sudo mv $HOME/drush /usr/share
   ```

3. Set proper permissions to the drush executable file:

   ```
   $ sudo chmod u+x /usr/share/drush/drush
   ```

4. Create a symbolic link of the Drush executable to any of the directories listed at your $PATH environment variable so that you do not have to type /usr/share/drush/drush every time you use it.

   ```
   $ echo $PATH
   /home/juampy/.composer/vendor/bin:/usr/local/sbin:
   ```

```
/usr/local/bin:/usr/sbin:/usr/bin:/sbin:/bin:/usr/games:
/usr/local/games
$ sudo ln -s /usr/share/drush/drush /usr/local/bin/drush
```

5. The next step consists of installing Composer dependencies for Drush:

```
$ cd /usr/share/drush
$ composer install
Loading composer repositories with package information
Installing dependencies (including require-dev) from lock file
 - Installing d11wtq/boris (v1.0.8)
 - Installing pear/console_table (1.1.5)
 - Installing phpunit/php-token-stream (1.2.2)
 - Installing symfony/yaml (v2.2.1)
 - Installing sebastian/version (1.0.3)
 - Installing sebastian/exporter (1.0.1)
 - Installing sebastian/environment (1.0.0)
 - Installing sebastian/diff (1.1.0)
 - Installing sebastian/comparator (1.0.0)
 - Installing phpunit/php-text-template (1.2.0)
 - Installing phpunit/phpunit-mock-objects (2.1.5)
 - Installing phpunit/php-timer (1.0.5)
 - Installing phpunit/php-file-iterator (1.3.4)
 - Installing phpunit/php-code-coverage (2.0.9)
 - Installing phpunit/phpunit (4.1.3)
 - Installing symfony/process (v2.4.5)
pear/console_table suggests installing pear/Console_Color
(>=0.0.4)
phpunit/phpunit suggests installing phpunit/php-invoker (~1.1)
Generating autoload files
```

6. Finally, verify the installation:

```
$ cd $HOME
$ which drush
/usr/local/bin/drush
$ drush --version
Drush Version   :  7.0.0-alpha5
```

The main README file at the Drush repository has a great section on POST-INSTALL tasks (https://github.com/drush-ops/drush#post-install) with additional information on configuring PHP and extra settings for environments such as MAMP. It's worth taking a look at it.

# The Drush command structure

Drush offers a broad list of commands that cover practically all the aspects of a Drupal project. If you are already fluent with executing commands in the terminal, you can skip this section. Otherwise, keep on reading to discover what arguments and options are and how these affect the behavior of a command.

We can view the available list of commands by running drush help. Additionally, running drush help some-command will show you detailed information about a particular command.

# Executing a command

Let's start with a very simple command such as core-status, which prints environment information about Drush and, if available, a Drupal site. Assuming that we have a Drupal project installed at /home/juampy/projects/drupal, let's run this command here and see its output:

```
$ drush core-status
 Drupal version            :  7.29-dev
 Site URI                  :  http://default
 Database driver           :  mysql
 Database username         :  root
 Database name             :  drupal7x
 Database                  :  Connected
 Drupal bootstrap          :  Successful
 Drupal user               :
 Default theme             :  bartik
 Administration theme      :  seven
 PHP executable            :  /usr/bin/php
 PHP configuration         :  /etc/php5/cli/php.ini
 PHP OS                    :  Linux
 Drush version             :  7.0.0-alpha5
 Drush temp directory      :  /tmp
```

```
Drush alias files              :
Drupal root                    :  /home/juampy/projects/drupal
Site path                      :  sites/default
File directory path            :  sites/default/files
Temporary file directory path  :  /tmp
```

The preceding output informs us about the main configuration of the Drupal project plus some Drush environment settings.

# Providing arguments to a command

The `core-status` command accepts a single argument that specifies which setting is to be retrieved (you can see this information by running `drush help core-status`). An argument is a string of text that acts as an input data for a command. Arguments are entered after the command name and are separated by spaces. Therefore, if we need to print just the items containing `version` in the setting name, we can execute the following command:

```
$ drush core-status version
 Drupal version  :  7.29-dev
 Drush version   :  7.0.0-alpha5
```

Drush commands might accept zero to any number of arguments depending on their nature. Beware that some commands expect arguments to be given in a certain order. For example, the `variable-set` command, used to change Drupal environment variables, requires the first argument to be the variable name and the second argument to be the variable's new value. Hence, the following example sets the `site-name` variable to the `My awesome site` value:

```
$ drush variable-set site-name "My awesome site"
site-name was set to "My awesome site".          [success]
```

# Altering a command's behavior through options

Drush commands might accept options through the command line, which alter their default behavior. Options are in the form of `--option-name` or `--option-name=value`. Additionally, some options have a shorter version. For example, you can accept all confirmations for a Drush command by appending `--yes` or its shorter version: `-y`.

Let's take a look at options with an example. The `core-status` command has an option to show the database password. We will now add it to the command and inspect the output:

```
$ cd /home/juampy/projects/drupal
$ drush core-status --show-passwords database
 Database driver     :   mysql
 Database username   :   root
 Database password   :   mysecretpw
 Database name       :   drupal7x
 Database            :   Connected
```

The `--show-passwords` option orders the `core-status` command that we want to see the database password of the Drupal site being bootstrapped.

# Structuring command invocations

Excluding some exceptions, there is no strict ordering for options and arguments when you run a command. Besides, Drush does a great job parsing arguments and options no matter how we mix them up in the input. However, our commands will be more readable if we follow this pattern:

```
$ drush [global options] [command name] [command options] [arguments]
```

Here is an example:

```
$ drush --verbose core-status --show-passwords database
```

And the following are the commands used in the previous example:

- `--verbose`: This is a Drush global option. You can see all the available global options by running `drush topic core-global-options`.
- `core-status`: This is the command that we are running.
- `--show-passwords`: This is an option of the `core-status` command.
- `database`: This is an argument for the `core-status` command.

Besides the fact of higher clarity by using the preceding structure, there are some commands in Drush that require options to be given in this order. This is the case of the `core-sync` Drush command, which is a wrapper of the actual Unix `rsync` command used to copy files and directories. Let's take a look at the following example:

```
$ drush rsync @self:%files/ /tmp/files --dry-run
You will destroy data from /tmp/files and replace with data from /home/
juampy/projects/drupal/sites/default/files/
Do you really want to continue? (y/n):
```

The preceding command copies files recursively from a Drupal project into `/tmp/files`. The `--dry-run` option is an `rsync` specific option that attempts to copy files but does not make any actual changes. Now, let's try to run the same command but this time placing the option before the command name:

```
$ drush --dry-run rsync @self:%files/ /tmp/files
```

```
Unknown option: --dry-run.  See `drush help core-rsync` for available
options. To suppress this error, add the option -strict=0.  [error]
```

We can see in the preceding output that Drush attempted to evaluate the `--dry-run` option and failed as it did not recognize it. This example demonstrates that you should carefully read the description of a command by running `drush help command-name` in order to understand its options, arguments, and ordering.

# Command aliases

Most of Drush commands support a shorter name to be used when invoking them. You can find them in parenthesis next to each command name when running `drush help`, or in the `Aliases` section when viewing the full help of a command.

For example, the `core-status` command can also be executed with `status` or just `st`, which means that the following commands will return identical results:

```
$ drush core-status
```

```
$ drush status
```

```
$ drush st
```

> For clarity, we will not use command aliases in this book, but these help us to work faster. So, it is worthwhile to use them.

# Understanding Drush's context system

Drush is decoupled from Drupal. This means that it does not necessarily need a Drupal site to work with. Some commands do require a Drupal project to bootstrap, while for others, this might be optional. Let's take `core-status` as an example. This command gives us information about the current context. If we run this command outside of a Drupal project, we will obtain configuration details for Drush and our local environment:

```
$ cd $HOME
```

```
$ drush core-status
```

```
PHP executable          :  /usr/bin/php
PHP configuration       :  /etc/php5/cli/php.ini
PHP OS                  :  Linux
Drush version           :  7.0.0-alpha5
Drush temp directory    :  /tmp
Drush alias files       :
```

Now, if we change directory to a Drupal project, we will get extra information about it:

```
$ cd /home/juampy/projects/drupal
$ drush core-status
  Drupal version              :  7.29-dev
  Site URI                    :  http://default
  Database driver             :  mysql
  Database username           :  root
  Database name               :  drupal7x
  Database                    :  Connected
  Drupal bootstrap            :  Successful
  Drupal user                 :
  Default theme               :  bartik
  Administration theme        :  seven
  PHP executable              :  /usr/bin/php
  PHP configuration           :  /etc/php5/cli/php.ini
  PHP OS                      :  Linux
  Drush version               :  7.0.0-alpha5
  Drush temp directory        :  /tmp
  Drush alias files           :
  Drupal root                 :  /home/juampy/projects/drupal
  Site path                   :  sites/default
  File directory path         :  sites/default/files
  Temporary file directory path :  /tmp
```

In the preceding scenario, Drush finds out that it is currently at the root of a Drupal project that uses the default location to store its settings (sites/default). Therefore, it is able to bootstrap Drupal and load its configuration.

# Setting the context manually

We do not have to be at the root of a Drupal project in order to run Drush commands against it. Instead, we can append additional options that will let Drush find it. For example, we could run the core-status command from a different directory, adding the --root option that points to the root of our Drupal project:

```
$ cd /home/juampy
$ drush --root=/home/juampy/projects/drupal core-status
 Drupal version            :   7.29-dev
 Site URI                  :   http://default
 Database driver           :   mysql
 Database username         :   root
 Database name             :   drupal7x
 Database                  :   Connected
 Drupal bootstrap          :   Successful
 Drupal root               :   /home/juampy/projects/drupal
 Site path                 :   sites/default
```

As we can see at the command output, Drush did bootstrap Drupal although we were not at its root directory. On a multisite Drupal installation, where settings. php is not at sites/default, we need to specify the site within our Drupal project that we want to bootstrap with the --uri option:

```
$ cd /home/juampy
$ drush --root=/home/juampy/projects/drupal --uri=mysite core-status
 Drupal version            :   7.29-dev
 Site URI                  :   other_site
 Database driver           :   mysql
 Database username         :   root
 Database name             :   other_site
 Database                  :   Connected
 Drupal bootstrap          :   Successful
```

```
Drupal root                 :   /home/juampy/projects/drupal
Site path                   :   sites/mysite
...
```

# Summary

This chapter was an introduction to the principles of Drush. We covered the installation requirements so that you could set them up on your local environment and then proceeded with the installation of Drush.

Next, we went through some command-line basics that involved how to invoke commands, and how to append options and arguments as well. We saw some caveats regarding the order of options and arguments and suggested a structure to construct command invocations that is easy to read.

The last section of the chapter gave some tips on how to set the context of a Drupal project for Drush. We saw that Drush is pretty intelligent and can automatically figure out whether we are on a Drupal project in order to bootstrap it, or we can alternatively pass extra options to inform where our Drupal project is.

In the next chapter, we will go through one of the most important challenges of developing Drupal projects and how Drush can help us with it: keeping configuration and code together.

# 2
# Keeping Database Configuration and Code Together

One of the most remarkable articles that I read when I started to learn Drupal is *The Development -> Staging -> Production Workflow Problem in Drupal* (`http://www.developmentseed.org/blog/2009/jul/09/development-staging-production-workflow-problem-drupal`), by Development Seed. Dated back to 2009, yet it still outlines, with such clarity, one of the most important challenges in Drupal projects; the fact that although a part of Drupal's configuration resides in the database and not in code, these must evolve together under a version control system such as Git.

This quote in particular really did hit me:

> *"The ideal development workflow involves communication in both directions. Content needs to be migrated upstream to staging and development servers, and configuration needs to be migrated downstream to staging and production."*

Let's dissect this:

*Content needs to be migrated upstream to staging and development servers...*

This means that the database should be copied from production to other environments (staging, development, and your local environment) on a regular basis in order to test code and configuration changes against recent content. This process helps you to verify that a copy of the production environment's database updates with new code as you would expect. This should eliminate surprises when deploying a new release to production.

Now, let's see the second statement:

*…configuration needs to be migrated downstream to staging and production.*

By configuration, the article refers to custom code plus exported configuration such as user roles, content types, fields, layouts, and so on. These two are pushed from your local environment downstream to other environments (development, staging, and production).

Both streams have something in common: either when we install the production environment's database on our local environment or when we deploy new code, the database needs to be updated. Updating means going through a list of steps that can be accomplished via Drupal's administration interface or using Drush. In this chapter, we will automate this process, which we will call the update path.

# Meeting the update path

The update path is a list of steps that update the database of a Drupal project so that it is in sync with the code.

Running the update path in a Drupal project involves the following steps:

1. Rebuilding Drupal's registry.
2. Running database updates.
3. Importing configuration.
4. Clearing caches.

In the following sections, we will dive deeper into each of the preceding steps. These can be accomplished manually with Drupal's administration interface. However, this is a tedious process. Ideally, we would like to make the deployment process as straightforward as possible, so here is how we can automate the preceding steps with Drush commands in a Bash script that we will save as /home/juampy/scripts/ update_path.sh:

```
#!/bin/sh
#
# Run the update path in the current project.
#
# Usage:
# Change directory into a Drupal project and run:
#    sh /path-to-this-script/update_path.sh
#
```

```
# You may need to change permissions on this script with the
following:
#    chmod u+x /path-to-this-script/update_path.sh

echo "Starting update path"

# 1. Registry Rebuild.
drush --verbose registry-rebuild --no-cache-clear
# 2. Run database updates.
drush --verbose --yes updatedb
# 3. Clear the Drush cache.
# Sometimes Features may need this due to a bug in Features module.
drush cache-clear drush
# 4. Revert all features.
drush --verbose --yes features-revert-all
# 5. Clear all caches.
drush --verbose cache-clear all
echo "Update path completed."
```

What we are doing in the preceding script is rebuilding some of the data structures that Drupal stores in the database from most generic to most specific. You would run this script when:

- You have just downloaded a copy of the production environment's database
- You have just pulled in the most recent version of the project's source code
- You have made changes in the site's configuration and want to revert them back
- You have just deployed a new release into a different environment (for example, staging)

Keeping configuration in sync with the code is critical in order to work within a team and to avoid unexpected results when deploying code to other environments.

All the commands in the script use the `--verbose` option. This helps us to verify that Drush is loading the right context, and if there are any PHP warnings or notices during the process, we will see them. The output generated when running the script is quite long because of the `--verbose` option, but at its simplest form, it would be like the following code:

```
$ cd /home/juampy/projects/drupal
$ sh /home/juampy/scripts/update_path.sh
Starting update path
There were 896 files in the registry before and 896 files now.
Registry has been rebuilt.                                       [success]
No database updates required                                     [success]
Current state already matches defaults, aborting.                    [ok]
'all' cache was cleared.                                         [success]
Update path completed.
```

In the preceding execution, the registry did not change, no database updates were run nor were features reverted. In the following sections, we will look into more detail on each of the steps of the update path in order to discover how to solve some of the challenges we might find when upgrading the database with new code.

# Rebuilding the registry

Drupal's registry system is an autoloading mechanism for PHP classes and interfaces. It keeps track of the location of the file that contains each class in order to load it whenever it is required. Classes can be autoloaded by listing them at the `files[]` section of the `.info` file of a module.

There are scenarios where Drupal enters in a deadlock caused by a missing class that is required during an early stage of the bootstrap process. You might face this error while upgrading a module or after moving an installed module into a different directory.

In the following sections, we will create a scenario where Drupal's registry will break and then fix it by running the `registry-rebuild` Drush command.

## Preparing the trap

*Beware! Proceed with the following steps on a testing environment.*

The trap to break Drupal's registry will consist of:

1.  Installing `Field collection` (https://www.drupal.org/project/field_collection) and `Entity` (https://drupal.org/project/entity) modules.

2. Adding a field of type `Field collection` to the `Page` content type.

3. Creating a node of type `Page`.

4. Moving the `Entity` module to a different location within the `sites/all/modules` directory.

Let's start by downloading and installing the `Field collection` module in a Drupal project:

```
$ cd /home/juampy/projects/drupal
$ drush pm-download field_collection
Project field_collection (7.x-1.0-beta7) downloaded to /.../sites/all/
modules/contrib/field_collection.                         [success]
$ drush --yes pm-enable field_collection
The following projects have unmet dependencies:
field_collection requires entity
Would you like to download them? (y/n): y
Project entity (7.x-1.5) downloaded to/.../sites/all/modules/contrib/
entity.                                                   [success]
Project entity contains 2 modules: entity_token, entity.
The following extensions will be enabled: field_collection, entity
Do you really want to continue? (y/n): y
entity was enabled successfully.                             [ok]
field_collection was enabled successfully.                   [ok]
```

Drush took care of downloading the dependency of `Field collection` on the `Entity` module and installed it automatically. Let's move on to the next step, where we will set up a scenario where Drupal's registry system will crash. We need to add a `Field collection` field to a content type (for example, the `Basic Page` content type). We can do so by opening a browser and navigating to **Structure | Content Types | Basic Page | Manage Fields**. Alternatively, we can run the following Drush command:

```
$ drush field-create page items,field_collection,field_collection_embed
http://default/admin/structure/types/manage/page/fields/items
```

The command returned a URL to further edit the field settings. We now need to create a node of type Basic Page. Open your browser and navigate to **Add Content | Basic Page**:

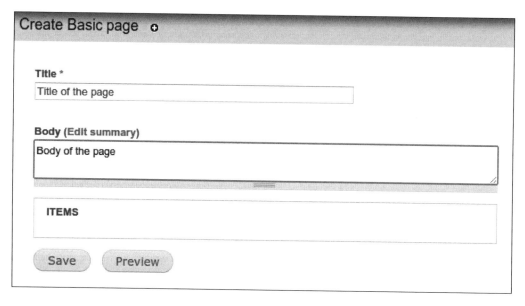

Once we click **Save**, we can see the page node's full display:

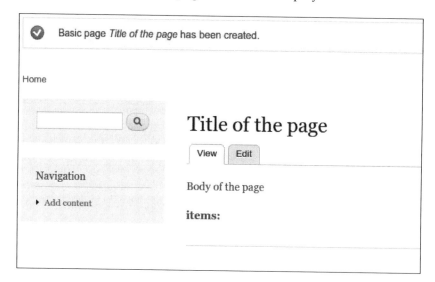

# Breaking the registry

Now, let's break the registry by moving the `Entity` module to a different location. Currently, it is installed at `sites/all/modules/contrib/entity`. We will move it to `sites/all/modules`, where Drupal should be able to find it too:

```
$ mv sites/all/modules/contrib/entity sites/default/modules/
```

After moving the `Entity` module and reloading the node page in the browser, we will see a PHP error that refers to the `Entity` class not being found:

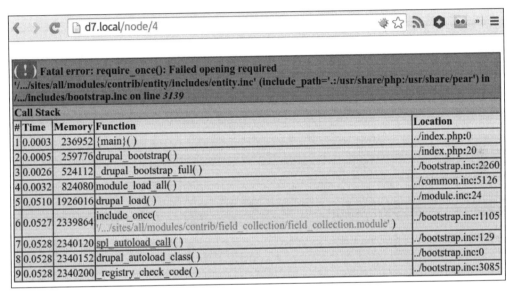

If we open other pages of our website, we will experience the same error. Normally, when we see an error like this in a Drupal project, the first thing we would try will be to clear all caches. However, in this case, this solution won't work as we will face the same error when Drush bootstraps Drupal:

```
$ drush cache-clear all
require_once(/.../sites/all/modules/contrib/entity/includes/entity.
inc):failed to open stream: No such file or directory          [warning]
```

# Rebuilding Drupal's registry

This is the time when `Registry Rebuild` kicks in to help. Let's first download it into `sites/all/drush/commands`. The reason for using this path and not `sites/all/modules/contrib` is that `Registry Rebuild` is not a module. It just implements a PHP script and a Drush command. By placing it at `sites/all/drush/command`, Drush can discover it automatically and it will be available when we deploy this project to other environments:

```
$ drush @none pm-download \
  --destination=sites/all/drush/commands registry_rebuild
The directory sites/all/drush/commands does not exist.
Would you like to create it? (y/n): y
Project registry_rebuild (7.x-2.2) downloaded to /.../sites/all/drush/
commands/registry_rebuild.                              [success]
Project registry_rebuild contains 0 modules: .
```

Note the use of `@none` right before the command name while downloading `Registry Rebuild`. The `@none` alias is a Drush site alias. In essence, a Drush alias contains an array that defines where a Drupal project is and how it can be accessed. The `@none` Drush site alias is a special one as it tells Drush not to attempt bootstrapping a Drupal project at all. We need `@none` in this case because if we don't use it, Drush would discover that our current directory is a Drupal project and would try to bootstrap it, thus crashing again. We will cover site aliases in *Chapter 5, Managing Local and Remote Environments*.

In the preceding output, Drush informs us that `Registry Rebuild` does not have any modules. However, it just implements the `registry-rebuild` command, which we will use now to fix Drupal's registry:

```
$ drush registry-rebuild
The registry has been rebuilt via registry_rebuild (A).          [success]
All caches have been cleared with drush_registry_rebuild_cc_all.
                                                                 [success]
The registry has been rebuilt via drush_registry_rebuild_cc_all (B).
                                                                 [success]
All caches have been cleared with drush_registry_rebuild_cc_all.
                                                                 [success]
All registry rebuilds have been completed.                       [success]
```

Now, if we open again the node page in our web browser or navigate through our Drupal site, we won't see any errors. The `drush cache-clear all` command will work as well.

It is safe to rebuild the registry as it ensures that Drupal can bootstrap successfully. This is the reason why it is executed in the first place at the update_path.sh script.

# Running database updates

Right after rebuilding the registry, the next thing that needs to be done to get code and configuration in sync is to run all pending database updates found in Drupal core, contributed, and custom modules. A database update can involve creating new tables to store field data, add indexes, populate existing data, and so on.

Creating a database update involves implementing hook_update_N() (https://api. drupal.org/api/drupal/modules%21system%21system.api.php/function/hook_ update_N/7). This hook has the following signature: hook_update_N(&$sandbox), where $sandbox is an array that keeps track of the state and progress of the database update. Let's see it in action with a practical example; imagine that we want to add a Boolean field to our Basic Page content type called Flag with a default value of 0 (zero). Here is Drupal's administration interface where we will add the field:

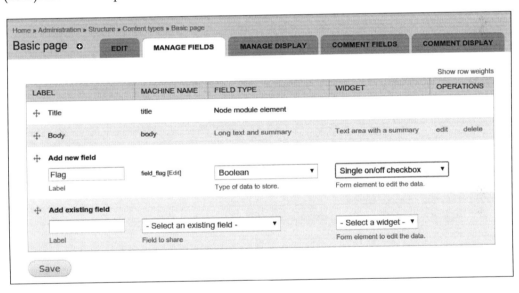

There is a problem with this setup; although the new content of type Page will have the Flag field set to zero, the existing content has a value of NULL because the table that stores data for our new Flag field is empty. This will cause the Views conditions or custom code that relies on the Flag field to be zero to return odd results. See the following SQL query, where we list the contents of the table containing data for the Flag field:

```
$ cd /home/juampy/projects/example
```

```
$ drush sql-cli
Welcome to the MySQL monitor.  Commands end with ; or \g.
mysql> select * from field_data_field_flag;
Empty set (0.00 sec)
```

Confirmed! There is no value for existing content at the `Flag` field. We need to write a database update that sets `field_flag = 0` on the existing content. Assuming that we have a custom module called `mymodule` already installed at `sites/all/modules/custom/mymodule`, here is a database update for `mymodule.install`:

```php
<?php
/**
 * @file
 *
 * Install hook implementations for module mymodule.
 */

/**
 * Set default value of 0 for field_flag on existing content.
 */
function mymodule_update_7100(&$sandbox) {
  // Load up all Basic Page nodes.
  $query = new EntityFieldQuery();
  $query->entityCondition('entity_type', 'node')
    ->entityCondition('bundle', 'page');
  $results = $query->execute();

  // Loop over each page node and set field_flag to 0.
  foreach (node_load_multiple(array_keys($results['node'])) as $node)
    {
    $node->field_flag[LANGUAGE_NONE][0]['value'] = 0;
    node_save($node);
  }
}
```

If you have a large amount of content, this database update should make use of the Batch API so that it can process nodes in chunks in order to avoid hitting memory limits or timeouts. Take a look at the **Code** section at `https://api.drupal.org/api/drupal/modules%21system%21system.api.php/function/hook_update_N/7` for further documentation.

Now, let's run database updates to see the database update in action:

```
$ drush --verbose updatedb
 Mymodule  7100  Set default value of 0 for field_flag on existing
content.
 Do you wish to run all pending updates? (y/n): y
 Executing mymodule_update_7100                                  [notice]
 Performed update: mymodule_update_7100                          [ok]
 'all' cache was cleared.                                        [success]
 Finished performing updates.                                    [ok]
```

Once we have run database updates, we can verify that the existing content has the right default values by inspecting the database:

```
$ drush sql-cli
Welcome to the MySQL monitor.  Commands end with ; or \g.
mysql> select entity_id, field_flag_value from field_data_field_flag;
+-----------+------------------+
| entity_id | field_flag_value |
+-----------+------------------+
|         1 |                0 |
|         2 |                0 |
|         3 |                0 |
|         4 |                0 |
+-----------+------------------+
```

We can see that each node has a value of 0 for the Flag field, which is what we initially wanted. Now that we know how to write and execute database updates in Drush, let's move on to the next step in the update path.

# Managing features

The Features module is the standard tool to export configuration into code for Drupal projects, so it can be under version control systems such as Git. The Features module is not perfect though and it can frustrate you at times until you understand how it works and its limitations (at least, that has been my personal experience with it so far). However, with the examples that we will see in this chapter, you will get a good understanding of it. Drush will be present throughout the whole process, of course.

There are two processes that we will use while working with the Features module:

- **Exporting configuration from the database into a module's code**: This can be achieved through the `features-export` command
- **Importing configuration components located in a module's code into the database**: This can be achieved through the `features-revert` command.

A common scenario involving these two processes is when you add a new field in your local environment and want this field to be installed in the development environment. You would export the field into the code at your local environment, then push your changes to the repository, and finally log in to the development environment to pull code changes and import the new configuration. Let's see the whole process with an example.

 Feature components can be safely exported into custom modules that already contain code in their module file.

# Exporting configuration into code

Let's start by taking the field we added in the previous section (`field_flag`) and export it into a custom module. The first thing to do is to download and install the Features module:

```
$ drush pm-download features
Project features (7.x-2.2) downloaded to/.../sites/all/modules/contrib/
features.                                                       [success]
$ drush --yes pm-enable features
The following extensions will be enabled: features
Do you really want to continue? (y/n): y
features was enabled successfully.                                  [ok]
```

Once the Features module has been installed, we can export the field into code. A field is composed of a field base, which contains the field definition and default settings, and a set of field instances. Each instance represents a field attached to an entity. In this case, we have one field base (`field_flag`) and one field instance (the Flag field attached to the Basic Page content type). We are going to export these two into the existing custom module `mymodule`. The first thing we need to do is to figure out the machine name of the field base:

```
$ drush features-components
Enter a number to choose which component type to list.
 [0]    : Cancel
```

```
    [1]   :   all
    [2]   :   dependencies
    [3]   :   field_base
    [4]   :   field_instance
    [5]   :   filter
    [6]   :   image
    [7]   :   menu_custom
    [8]   :   menu_links
    [9]   :   node
    [10]  :   taxonomy
    [11]  :   user_permission
    [12]  :   user_role
    [13]  :   views_view
3
Available sources
field_base:body
field_base:field_flag
field_base:comment_body
field_base:field_tags
field_base:field_image
```

We found it. `field_base:field_flag` is the field base of our `Flag` field. Let's export it into the module `mymodule`:

```
$ drush features-export mymodule field_base:field_flag
Module located at sites/all/modules/custom/mymodule will be updated. Do
you want to continue? (y/n): y
Created module: mymodule in sites/all/modules/custom/mymodule      [ok]
```

Now, we will repeat the operation for the field instance of `Flag`:

```
$ drush features-components
Enter a number to choose which component type to list.
    [0]   :   Cancel
    [1]   :   all
    [2]   :   dependencies
    [3]   :   field_base
    [4]   :   field_instance
    [5]   :   filter
```

```
[6]     :   image
[7]     :   menu_custom
[8]     :   menu_links
[9]     :   node
[10]    :   taxonomy
[11]    :   user_permission
[12]    :   user_role
[13]    :   views_view
4
Available sources
field_instance:comment-comment_node_article-comment_body
field_instance:comment-comment_node_page-comment_body
field_instance:node-article-body
field_instance:node-article-field_image
field_instance:node-article-field_tags
field_instance:node-page-body
```
**field_instance:node-page-field_flag**

Gotcha, the field instance is called `field_instance:node-page-field_flag`. Now, we can export it into the module `mymodule`:

```
$ drush features-export mymodule field_instance:node-page-field_flag
Module located at sites/all/modules/custom/mymodule will be updated. Do
you want to continue? (y/n): y
Created module: mymodule in sites/all/modules/custom/mymodule        [ok]
```

That's it. Now, we have the field base and field instance of the `Flag` field exported into code. Let's move on to the next step.

The user interface to export the feature components is more user friendly than the command-line interface; so, when in doubt, open it in a browser by navigating to **Structure | Features | Create / Recreate** and then select which components you want to export. Importing configuration into the database.

Let's try to delete the **Flag** field in our local environment and then run **features-revert** on the module **mymodule** so that its configuration gets imported into the database. The result should be that the `Flag` field gets reinstalled:

```
$ drush field-delete field_flag
Do you want to delete the field_flag field? (y/n): y
```

Drush has deleted the `Flag` field. We will now list the available fields to verify that `field_flag` is not present:

```
$ drush field-info fields
 Field name      Field type
 comment_body    text_long
 body            text_with_summary
 field_tags      taxonomy_term_reference
 field_image     image
```

It is now confirmed that `field_flag` is not listed in the preceding code. Now, we will revert the module `mymodule`, so the exported `Flag` field that it contains gets installed back into the database again:

```
$ drush features-revert mymodule
Do you really want to revert mymodule.field_base? (y/n): y
Reverted mymodule.field_base.                                    [ok]
Do you really want to revert mymodule.field_instance? (y/n): y
Reverted mymodule.field_instance.                               [ok]
```

Finally, let's list again the available fields in the database:

```
$ drush field-info fields
 Field name      Field type
 comment_body    text_long
 body            text_with_summary
 field_tags      taxonomy_term_reference
 field_image     image
 field_flag      list_boolean
```

As we can see, in the preceding output, the field has been installed in our database. This was, at the bare minimum, the process of exporting and then importing configuration using the `Features` module. This strategy is used to apply new configuration in other environments, which is what we will do in the following section: *Running the update path on a different environment*.

The examples that we covered so far in this chapter taught us to write database updates and export configuration into a module. This should be enough insight to deploy our code into a different environment (for example, the development environment), and then run the `updatepath.sh` script in order to import the new configuration.

# Running the update path on a different environment

So far in this chapter, we created a `Flag` field, exported it to an existing custom module called `mymodule`, and then wrote a database update that sets its default value to zero on the existing content. Let's suppose that we have committed this code to a version control system such as Git and then deployed it
to the development environment, where:

- Drush is installed

- The `Features` module is installed in the Drupal project

- The custom module `mymodule` was installed, but it did not have the new code that we just deployed

- The script that contains the update path is located at `/var/www/exampledev/update_path.sh`

If we run the update path script on this environment, we should expect the `Flag` field to be added and set to zero for the existing content. Let's run it to see if we are right:

```
(Development) $ cd /var/www/exampledev/docroot
(Development) $ sh -x ../update_path.sh
Starting update path for 'current site'
```

We have initiated the execution of the update path script. We added the `-x` flag so that we can see each command within `update_path.sh` being executed and listed in the following output with a plus sign at the start of the line:

```
+ drush --verbose registry-rebuild
The registry has been rebuilt via registry_rebuild (A).        [success]
All caches have been cleared with drush_registry_rebuild_cc_all.
                                                               [success]
The registry has been rebuilt via drush_registry_rebuild_cc_all (B).
                                                               [success]
There were 139 files in the registry before and 139 files now.    All
caches have been cleared with drush_registry_rebuild_cc_all.   [success]
All registry rebuilds have been completed.                     [success]
```

The first step was completed and the registry has been rebuilt. Now, let's see the database update in action:

```
+ drush --verbose --yes updatedb
```

```
Mymodule   7100   Set default value of 0 for field_flag on existing
content.
Do you wish to run all pending updates? (y/n): y
Executing mymodule_update_7100
Performed update: mymodule_update_7100                        [ok]
'all' cache was cleared.                                  [success]
+ drush --verbose cache-clear drush
'drush' cache was cleared.                                [success]
```

Our custom database update was completed successfully. Now, it's time to revert the exported components with the Features module:

```
+ drush --verbose --yes features-revert-all
The following modules will be reverted: mymodule
Do you really want to continue? (y/n): y
Reverted mymodule.field_base.                                 [ok]
Reverted mymodule.field_instance.                            [ok]
```

The Features module found new components in the module mymodule and imported them; so, the new Flag field has been created. We complete the process by moving on to the last step that consists of clearing all caches:

```
+ drush --verbose --yes cache-clear all
'all' cache was cleared.                                  [success]
+ echo Update path completed.
Update path completed.
```

# Analyzing results

The update path was completed successfully. Let's check whether the Flag field has been created:

```
(Development) $ drush field-info fields
Field name      Field type
comment_body    text_long
body            text_with_summary
field_tags      taxonomy_term_reference
field_image     image
field_flag      list_boolean
```

This is correct. The `Flag` field exists in the database. Now, let's make sure that the existing content has the correct default value:

```
(Development) $ drush sql-cli
Welcome to the MySQL monitor.  Commands end with ; or \g.
mysql> select * from field_data_field_flag;
Empty set (0.00 sec)
```

Wait! Why does the existing content not have the `Flag` field set to zero when we ran this same database update in our local environment? The reason is that the update path script runs database updates before importing configuration, so by the time our database update was executed, the `Flag` field was not installed yet. In the following section, we will fix this by programmatically installing the field during the database update.

We could alter the update path script so that it runs `drush features-revert-all` before running database updates, but this would make it impossible to make changes in the database before importing a new configuration.

# Reverting the feature components programmatically

As we saw in the previous section, there are cases where we need to import configuration manually before we run database updates. Therefore, we will add a new database update to the module `mymodule` where we do the following:

- Import the `Flag` field configuration located at module `mymodule`
- Make sure that the field is created and throws an error otherwise
- Set a default value for this field for the existing content

Here is `sites/all/modules/custom/mymodule/mymodule.install` with the new database update:

```php
<?php
/**
 * @file
 *
 * Install hook implementations for module mymodule.
 */

/**
 * Dummy database update.
```

```
  */
function mymodule_update_7100(&$sandbox) {
  // This database update failed so we have moved the code
  // to the next database update with a few adjustments.
}

/**
 * Set default value of 0 for field_flag on existing content.
 */
function mymodule_update_7101(&$sandbox) {
  // Import field Flag into the database.
  $items['mymodule'] = array('field_base', 'field_instance');
  features_revert($items);

  // Make sure that the field Flag has been installed.
  if (empty(field_info_instance('node', 'field_flag', 'page'))) {
    $t_args = array('@function' => __FUNCTION__);
    throw new DrupalUpdateException(t('Field flag was not found in
      update @function.', $t_args));
  }

  // Load up all Basic Page nodes.
  $query = new EntityFieldQuery();
  $query->entityCondition('entity_type', 'node')
    ->entityCondition('bundle', 'page');
  $results = $query->execute();
  // Loop over each Page node and set field_flag to 0.
  foreach (node_load_multiple(array_keys($results['node'])) as
    $node) {
    $node->field_flag[LANGUAGE_NONE][0]['value'] = 0;
    node_save($node);
  }
}
```

We removed code at `mymodule_update_7100()` as it failed and then added a new database update at `mymodule_update_7101()` where it first installs the `Flag` field before we work with it. Now, we can push this database update to the development environment. Once the code is here, we can run the update path script again:

```
(Development) $ cd /var/www/exampledev/docroot

(Development) $ sh ../scripts/update_path.sh

Starting update path.

...
```

```
Executing mymodule_update_7101                                    [notice]
WD features: Revert completed for mymodule / field_base.          [notice]
WD features: Revert completed for mymodule / field_instance.      [notice]
Performed update: mymodule_update_7101                                [ok]
...
Update path completed.
```

As we can see, in the preceding code, the feature components in the module
`mymodule` were imported during the database update, thus installing the `Flag` field.
The following code confirmed that the `Flag` field was created:

```
// Make sure that the field Flag has been installed.
if (empty(field_info_instance('node', 'field_flag', 'page'))) {
  $t_args = array('@function' => __FUNCTION__);
  throw new DrupalUpdateException(t('Field flag was not found in
    update @function.', $t_args));
}
```

We can finally verify that the existing content has the default value of `0` for the
`Flag` field:

```
(Development) $ drush sql-cli
Welcome to the MySQL monitor.  Commands end with ; or \g.
mysql> select entity_id, field_flag_value from field_data_field_flag;
+-----------+------------------+
| entity_id | field_flag_value |
+-----------+------------------+
|         8 |                0 |
|         9 |                0 |
|        10 |                0 |
|        11 |                0 |
|        12 |                0 |
|        13 |                0 |
+-----------+------------------+
6 rows in set (0.00 sec)
```

Yippee! The field has been installed and it has the right value for the existing content.

# Summary

Keeping code and configuration together is one of the most important challenges in a Drupal project. In this chapter, we covered a strategy to accomplish this challenge, using a script that we called the update path. Next, we went through each of its steps in detail, explaining some useful scenarios in order to gain further insight into what these are meant to accomplish.

We started by explaining what Drupal's registry is and how to make sure that it does not break while bootstrapping, using the `registry-rebuild` Drush command. We actually broke the registry of a sample Drupal project and demonstrated how `Registry Rebuild` can get it back to work.

The next step in the update path discussed running database updates. We wrote a custom database update on a module and then executed it using Drush. The last step on the update path consisted of importing configuration using the `Features` module. Thanks to the `Features` module, we are able to export all sorts of configuration from a Drupal project into code, so it can be under version control and then deployed in other environments.

In the next chapter, we will dive into running tasks in Drupal projects. Drush has a lot of tools in its belt for this, which we will discover through practical examples.

# 3
# Running and Monitoring Tasks in Drupal Projects

Looking at Wikipedia for the definition of a task (`http://en.wikipedia.org/wiki/Task`), I found two of them. Here they are:

- *In project management, an activity that needs to be accomplished within a defined period of time*
- *In computing, a program execution context*

Some examples of tasks in Drupal projects are clearing caches, indexing content into a search engine, or importing content from a third-party API. These can be classified in the following types:

- **One-off**: This includes Drupal's database updates
- **On demand**: This includes reindexing all content in Apache Solr
- **Periodic**: This would be the case of Drupal's cron

Drush is really good at running long tasks in an isolated process. It supports both Batch and Queue APIs, so the workload can be either split into batches or workers, respectively. In this chapter, we will see some tips and examples of best practices to run tasks against a Drupal project using Drush. Here are the main topics:

- Running periodic tasks with cron
- Running a task outside cron
- Running long tasks in batches
- Evaluating code on the fly and running scripts
- Logging messages in Drush
- Redirecting Drush output into a file
- Running a command in the background

# Running periodic tasks with cron

The first place to go to set up periodic tasks is Drupal's cron (`https://www.drupal.org/cron`). Cron is a built-in tool that runs periodically to perform tasks such as clearing caches, checking for updates, or indexing content subject to be searched. Modules can implement `hook_cron()` (`https://api.drupal.org/api/drupal/modules%21system%21system.api.php/function/hook_cron/7`) in order to have their tasks executed via cron.

Drupal's default behavior is to run cron automatically every three hours. It can also be triggered manually through the administration interface or using Drush. Running cron with Drush is desirable for the following reasons:

- Drush runs using a different `PHP.ini` configuration than the web server that does not have a request timeout. Furthermore, other PHP variables such as `memory_limit` can be adjusted to higher values, if needed.

- Cron's output can be logged in to a file and monitored, so actions can be taken if there is an error.

- Drush can easily trigger cron on remote Drupal sites.

It is desirable to evaluate which tasks run in Drupal's cron and how often it runs. Here are some examples of what could happen if you don't keep an eye on this:

- If cron takes too long to complete, it won't run at the frequency that you set it to and tasks will pile up.

- If cron has to run tasks A, B, and C, and if task B provokes a PHP error, the whole process will terminate and task C won't be processed. This gets worse over time if the PHP error keeps happening on successive runs as task C won't be processed until the error is fixed.

# Disabling Drupal's cron

Drupal has a mechanism to trigger cron automatically by injecting a small piece of AJAX within a client's response, which makes a request to `http://mysite.example.com/cron.php?cron_key=some_token`. If we are about to trigger Drupal's cron exclusively through Drush, then we should disable this.

# Verifying the current cron frequency

The Drupal variable that defines how often cron should be triggered is called `cron_safe_threshold`. This variable has a default value in Drupal's source code of `10800` seconds (3 hours) while Drush hardcodes it to `0`. Let's check the current value of the variable in a clean Drupal project:

```
$ cd /home/juampy/projects/drupal
$ drush variable-get cron_safe_threshold
cron_safe_threshold: 0
```

We see that it has a value of `0`. However, this time, Drush is fooling us as it hardcodes it to `0` while bootstrapping Drupal. Drupal's variables are first searched in the `variable` table of the database and then they can be overridden via the global `$conf` variable (this is normally done in `settings.php`). Let's look for this variable in the database to see whether it has a value:

```
$ cd /home/juampy/projects/drupal
$ drush sql-cli
Welcome to the MySQL monitor.  Commands end with ; or \g.
mysql> select value from variable where name = 'cron_safe_threshold';
Empty set (0.00 sec)
mysql> exit
Bye
```

Gotcha! The variable does not exist in the database. Let's open the **Cron** settings page at Drupal's administration interface to see what is set there:

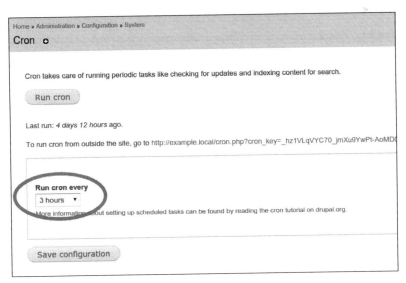

As we can see, it is set to **3 hours**. The reason is that Drupal requests the value for this field from the Drupal variable `cron_safe_threshold`. If this variable is not set, it defaults to the constant `DRUPAL_CRON_DEFAULT_THRESHOLD`, which has a value of 3 hours. Here is the line of code in Drupal core for this particular page:

```
# ./modules/system/system.admin.inc:1634:
'#default_value' => variable_get('cron_safe_threshold',
  DRUPAL_CRON_DEFAULT_THRESHOLD),
```

## Overriding cron frequency and exporting it to code

Now, we will set this variable to 0 in the database and then export it into code with the `Features` module, which we have already installed in the previous chapter. In order to export Drupal variables into code, we need to download and install the `Strongarm` module (https://www.drupal.org/project/strongarm):

```
$ drush pm-download strongarm
Project strongarm (7.x-2.0) downloaded
  to sites/all/modules/contrib/strongarm.                    [success]
$ drush --yes pm-enable strongarm
The following extensions will be enabled: strongarm, ctools
Do you really want to continue? (y/n): y
strongarm was enabled successfully.                               [ok]
ctools was enabled successfully.                                  [ok]
```

Next, let's set the value of the `cron_safe_threshold` variable to 0 in the database:

```
$ drush variable-set cron_safe_threshold 0
cron_safe_threshold was set to "0".                          [success]
```

Next, we will check whether the right value has been set in the database. Remember that when we looked for it before, the value did not exist in the `variable` table:

```
$ drush sql-cli
Welcome to the MySQL monitor.  Commands end with ; or \g.
mysql> select value from variable where name = 'cron_safe_threshold';
+----------+
| value    |
+----------+
| s:1:"0"; |
+----------+
1 row in set (0.00 sec)
```

That's correct. We now have the right value in the database as a serialized string, therefore, we can export it into code. The `Features` module classifies Drupal configuration into component types such as `field_base`, `image`, or `user_role`. The `features-components` command lists all available components to be exported. Let's figure out the component's machine name for the `cron_safe_threshold` variable:

```
$ drush features-components
Enter a number to choose which component type to list.
  [0]   :   Cancel
  [1]   :   all
  [2]   :   dependencies
  [3]   :   field_base
  [4]   :   field_instance
  [5]   :   filter
  [6]   :   image
  [7]   :   menu_custom
  [8]   :   menu_links
  [9]   :   node
  [10]  :   taxonomy
  [11]  :   user_permission
  [12]  :   user_role
  [13]  :   variable
13
Available sources
variable:admin_theme
variable:clean_url
variable:comment_page
variable:cron_key
variable:cron_last
variable:cron_safe_threshold
variable:css_js_query_string
  . . .
```

We found it. The component machine name is `variable:cron_safe_threshold`. As this is a site-wide setting, we will create a new module called `mysite` and store the variable here. This module can also accommodate site-wide custom code:

```
$ drush features-export mysite variable:cron_safe_threshold
Will create a new module in sites/all/modules/mysite
Do you really want to continue? (y/n): y
Created module: mysite in sites/all/modules/mysite      [ok]
```

Now, we can commit these changes into our version control system and deploy them into other environments, so that Drupal won't run cron automatically once the configuration has been imported with the `features-revert` command. We are now ready to set up cron with Drush, which we will cover in the following section.

# Running cron with Drush

This is how we can run cron with Drush:

```
$ cd /home/juampy/projects/drupal
$ drush core-cron
Cron run successful.                                    [success]
```

Some cron tasks, such as indexing content with Apache Solr's search engine, need to know the current hostname. Drush is unable to figure this out by itself, so we will provide this information with the `--uri` option, as in the following example:

```
$ drush --uri=http://d7.local core-cron
Cron run successful.                                    [success]
```

# Scheduling cron runs with Jenkins

There are several ways to run cron periodically with Drush. The most common ones are:

- Using Linux's crontab (`http://en.wikipedia.org/wiki/Cron`), a command-line job scheduler
- Using a Continuous Integration system such as Jenkins (`http://jenkins-ci.org`)

For the former, there is plenty of documentation within the `drush topic docs-cron` command, so we won't cover this option although it is worth reading it. The latter has the benefit that it provides a web interface that makes it very easy to monitor and trigger alerts, such as sending an e-mail when Drupal cron fails. In the following section, we will set up Jenkins to run Drupal's cron.

## Installing Jenkins

Jenkins can run jobs in the local environment where it is installed and in remote environments, providing a set of SSH credentials (`http://en.wikipedia.org/wiki/Secure_Shell`). In this case, we will go for the simplest possible example; we will install Jenkins in our local environment to trigger cron for our Drupal project.

The installation process for Jenkins varies depending on the operating system, so refer to the official documentation at `https://wiki.jenkins-ci.org/display/JENKINS/Installing+Jenkins` in order to get it working.

Once the installation is complete, open `http://localhost:8080` in your web browser and proceed to create the job that will run Drupal's cron.

## Creating a job through the web interface

We will now create and configure the job that will run and monitor Drupal's cron runs. Let's start by clicking on **New Item** in the top-left corner of the web interface and fill in the form to create our new job:

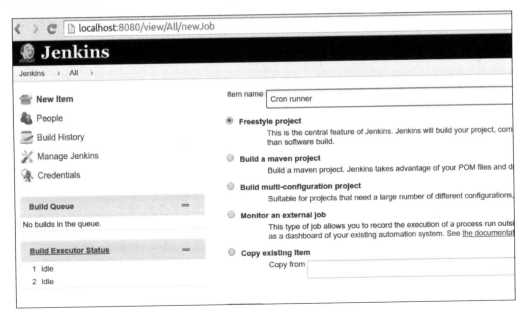

We have called our job Cron runner and chose the **Freestyle project** type. Once we submit the form, we are redirected to the job settings form. The first thing we want to set is how often this job will run. In the following screenshot, we will set it to run every two hours:

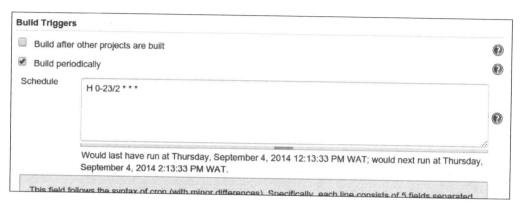

The syntax used to define the frequency of execution is very similar to the one for crontab. This syntax is flexible but tricky, so to make sure we got it right, Jenkins prints a human-readable version of what we entered right under the Schedule text area.

The next section to complete in this form is to add **Build** steps to the job. For this, we will have just one build step that will consist of running a few commands in order to run Drupal's cron through Drush. The following screenshot illustrates this:

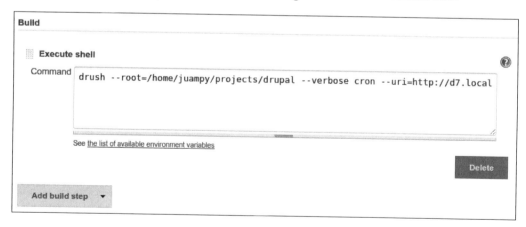

If there are any errors in the preceding step when the job is running, Jenkins will notice them as it will evaluate the output. This is useful for the following section that we will configure: **Post-build Actions**. We will add an action here to be notified via e-mail if a build fails:

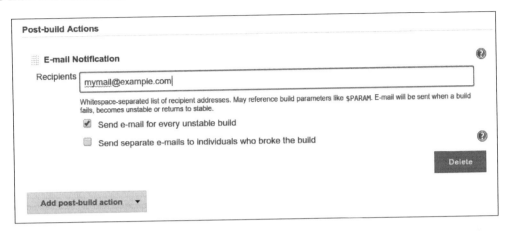

We are done setting up our Jenkins job. We can now click on **Save** and build the job manually by clicking on **Build Now** on the left sidebar to test it. Here is the output of the job:

```
Started by user anonymous
[EnvInject] - Loading node environment variables.
[EnvInject] - Preparing an environment for the build.
[EnvInject] - Keeping Jenkins system variables.
[EnvInject] - Keeping Jenkins build variables.
[EnvInject] - Injecting contributions.
Building in workspace /var/lib/jenkins/jobs/Cron runner/workspace
[workspace] $ /bin/sh -xe /tmp/hudson1449097994163880172.sh
+ cd /home/juampy/projects/drupal
+ /usr/share/drush/drush --verbose cron --uri=http://d7.local
Initialized Drupal 7.29-dev root directory at
   /home/juampy/projects/drupal                              [notice]
Initialized Drupal site d7.local at sites/default            [notice]
Indexing node 316.                                              [ok]
Cron run successful.                                        [success]
Finished: SUCCESS
```

As we can see from the preceding output, it is like running the command directly. Now, we can let Jenkins take care of running cron for us from now on.

# Monitoring cron runs

Jenkins will keep a list of past builds with all its related information such as input parameters, start and end time, output, and some useful statistics that will help you figure out the status of the job:

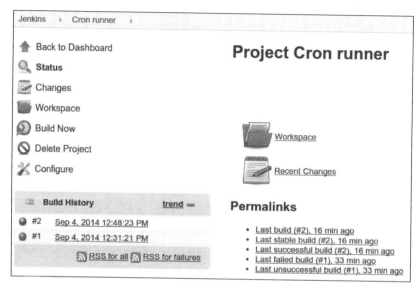

This was just a basic example of how to set up a Jenkins job to run Drupal's cron with Drush. Jenkins has a huge community that maintains a long list of plugins that extend its functionality. You can browse them at the official website (`https://wiki.jenkins-ci.org/display/JENKINS/Plugins`) or by navigating to **Manage Jenkins | Manage Plugins** through the administration interface of your Jenkins installation.

# Running a task outside cron

So far in this chapter, we have seen how to disable Drupal's automatic cron and how to schedule it to be run by Drush. Now, we have got to the point where we can evaluate whether there are any tasks running at cron in our Drupal project that should be moved out of it.

Here are the reasons why a task that runs within hook_cron() (https://api.
drupal.org/api/drupal/modules%21system%21system.api.php/function/
hook_cron/7) might need to be moved to its own process:

- The task might take a variable time to complete; sometimes, it will run in a couple of seconds, whereas for others, it might take an hour

- You want to run the task manually if you need to, and enter different input parameters depending on the circumstances

- The task's runtime log is highly valuable; therefore, it has to be saved into a different logfile with its own purging strategy

Whatever the reason, you can run any code within a custom Drush command and then schedule its processing through any of the methods mentioned in the previous section.

# Example – moving a Feeds importer from Drupal's cron to Drush

Modules add their tasks to Drupal's cron through hook_cron(). The Feeds module (https://www.drupal.org/project/feeds), for example, can import content from external sources with cron. Let's suppose that we have a Feeds importer that reads BBC's World Service RSS feed (http://feeds.bbci.co.uk/news/world/rss.xml) and creates articles in our Drupal site. We initially configured the Feeds importer to run within Drupal's cron, but for now, we want to create a Drush command that triggers it so that we can run this process out of hook_cron() in an independent process.

# Exporting the Feeds importer into code

The first thing that we should do is to disable the Feeds importer from running in cron. Here is what the main settings of our feed look like in Drupal's administration interface:

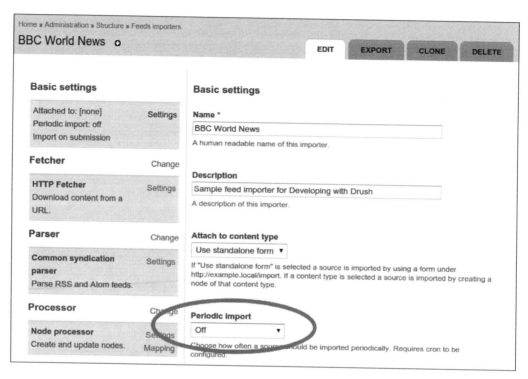

Now, in order to have everything in one module, we will export the Feeds importer into code and then write a custom Drush command to trigger it from the command line. In order to export the Feeds importer, we need to figure out its component machine name with the Features module:

```
$ drush features-components
Enter a number to choose which component type to list.
  [0]   :   Cancel
  [1]   :   all
  [2]   :   dependencies
  [3]   :   feeds_importer
  [4]   :   field_base
  [5]   :   field_instance
```

```
[6]    :   filter

[7]    :   image

[8]    :   menu_custom

[9]    :   menu_links

[10]   :   node

[11]   :   taxonomy

[12]   :   user_permission

[13]   :   user_role

[14]   :   variable

[15]   :   views_view

3

Available sources

feeds_importer:bbc_world_news

feeds_importer:node                 Provided by: feeds_import

feeds_importer:opml                 Provided by: feeds_news

feeds_importer:user                 Provided by: feeds_import
```

The Feeds importer's machine name is feeds_importer:bbc_world_news. We can now export it to a new custom module:

```
$ drush features-export newsfetcher \
  --destination=sites/all/modules/custom feeds_importer:bbc_world_news
Will create a new module in sites/all/modules/custom/newsfetcher
Do you really want to continue? (y/n): y
Created module: newsfetcher in sites/all/modules/custom/newsfetcher
[ok]
```

# Writing a Drush command to trigger the Feeds importer

When we exported the feed into code, we created a custom module: newsfetcher. We will now add a custom Drush command at sites/all/modules/custom/ newsfetcher/newsfetcher.drush.inc that will take care of triggering the import process. Here are its contents:

```
/**
 * Implements hook_drush_command().
 *
 * Defines the command to fetch news.
 */
```

```
function newsfetcher_drush_command() {
  $items = array();
  $items['news-fetch'] = array(
    'description' => "Fetches latest news from BBC's RSS feed.",
  );
  return $items;
}
```

The preceding code uses the bare minimum settings to define a Drush command. The following function is the command implementation:

```
/**
 * Implements drush_hook_COMMAND().
 *
 * Callback for news-fetch Drush command.
 */
function drush_newsfetcher_news_fetch() {
  // Load the Feeds importer.
  $source = feeds_source('bbc_world_news');

  // Set the import URL.
  $fetcher_config = $source->getConfigFor($source->importer-
    >fetcher);
  $fetcher_config['source'] =
    'http://feeds.bbci.co.uk/news/world/rss.xml';
  $source->setConfigFor($source->importer->fetcher,
    $fetcher_config);
  $source->save();

  // Execute the import.
  $source->startImport();
}
```

In order to test our new command, let's install our newsfetcher module and then run it to see its result:

```
$ drush pm-enable newsfetcher
The following extensions will be enabled: newsfetcher
Do you really want to continue? (y/n): y
newsfetcher was enabled successfully.                          [ok]
$ drush news-fetch
Created 55 nodes.                                          [status]
```

That's it! Now, we can run this task either manually or by scheduling it through crontab or any other job scheduling mechanism. As we just saw, the process of moving a task out of cron consists of figuring out how the task integrates with Drupal's cron, then disabling this integration, and finally writing a custom Drush command that triggers the task.

If you want to read further on how to write custom Drush commands, take a look at the Drush documentation by running `drush topic docs-commands` and `drush topic docs-examplecommand`. The `drushify` command is a very helpful resource too as it creates a template command file for a given module (`https://www.drupal.org/project/drushify`).

# Running long tasks in batches

There might be times where a task (for example, a Drush command or a PHP script) might take so long to complete that it hits one of PHP's constraints such as `memory_limit`, `max_execution_time`, or `max_input_vars`. In these cases, when you foresee that a task might take a considerable amount of time or resources to complete, it is safer to split the work into chunks that can be completed in smaller, independent, and consecutive processes. This is what Drupal's Batch API (`https://www.drupal.org/node/180528`) is for. In this section, we will explain how it works and examine how a contributed module uses it in order to complete a large task safely.

The most common errors we might find during a long process are:

- `Allowed memory size of [some number] bytes exhausted`: This means that our script attempted to use more memory than the maximum allowed to PHP at the `memory_limit` setting.

- `Fatal error: Maximum execution time of 30 seconds exceeded`: This means that our script took longer than the maximum amount of seconds defined by the PHP setting `max_execution_time`.

- `MySQL server has gone away`: This happens when we hit a timeout in the MySQL server. It can be provoked for various reasons (`http://dev.mysql.com/doc/refman/5.0/en/gone-away.html`) and sometimes can be fixed by adjusting `my.cnf`, but in essence, this is just another symptom of the fact that our process is trying to accomplish too much in just one go.

Drupal's Batch API is tricky. The real challenge is not that the API is badly architected, but that you need to make sure that the code that will run on each pass does not hit any PHP constraint.

This book won't cover Queue API. If you are interested, you can research its API reference section at `https://api.drupal.org/api/drupal/modules!system!system.queue.inc/group/queue/7`.

# A sample Drush command using the Batch API

Content revisioning is one of the most powerful features of Drupal. It gives editors the chance to edit a node and, if they are unhappy with their edits, they can roll back to a previous version of the content. The drawback of this feature is that the database size can grow quite quickly in certain scenarios. Here are a couple of them:

- A particular set of nodes is constantly being updated by editors; thus, the amount of revisions for them can grow up to hundreds or even thousands, which affects its performance

- A `Feeds` importer that runs periodically updates a long list of nodes on every run, generating new revisions for these nodes, which would increase the database size considerably over time

There might be some cases when we realize that we do not even need revisioning for a given content type. If this is the case, we can switch it off at the content type settings (warning, you will still need to delete old revisions of the existing content in order to recover the database space). In other content types such as `Page` and `Article`, you might prefer to keep the latest 10 revisions and automatically delete the older ones.

The `Node Revision Delete` module (`https://www.drupal.org/project/node_revision_delete`) is a contributed module used to delete old revisions of content. It can perform this task periodically through Drupal's cron or can be triggered through the administration interface or Drush. When run from Drupal's cron, it will just delete a few revisions. When triggered through the administration interface or Drush, it will delete all the older revisions of the selected content types. The latter can be quite a lengthy process on databases with a lot of revisions.

The following is the approach of the `Node Revision Delete` module: you first run the Drush command in order to do an initial, long, content revision pruning. Then, through the administration interface, you configure the module; so on every cron run, it evaluates whether it has to delete revisions from a list of selected content types.

Here is the command implementation. Note the use of the Batch API in order to prepare the job:

```
// http://cgit.drupalcode.org/node_revision_delete/
   tree/node_revision_delete.drush.inc#n37
/**
 * Implements drush_COMMANDFILE_COMMANDNAME().
 */
function drush_node_revision_delete($content_type,
  $revisions_to_keep) {
  // Set up the batch job.
  $batch = array(
    'operations' => array(
      array('node_revision_delete_batch_process', array($content_type,
$revisions_to_keep))
    ),
    'title' => t('Node Revision Delete batch job'),
    'init_message' => t('Starting...'),
    'error_message' => t('An error occurred'),
    'finished' => 'node_revision_delete_batch_finish',
    'file' => drupal_get_path('module', 'node_revision_delete') .
      '/node_revision_delete.batch.inc',
  );

  // Start the batch job.
  batch_set($batch);
  drush_backend_batch_process();
}
```

A batch job defines an array of `operations` to run (these are the ones that will do the actual processing) and a `finished` callback (the one that will evaluate results at the end and render a report). In this case, these are `node_revision_delete_batch_process` and `node_revision_delete_batch_finish`, respectively. Let's see them in detail.

# Batch API operations

An operation within a batch set is composed of a callback function plus a list of parameters needed by this callback. We define this while setting up the batch job in the following lines:

```
'operations' => array(
  array('node_revision_delete_batch_process',
    array($content_type, $revisions_to_keep))
),
```

The `node_revision_delete_batch_process` callback takes care of the following functions:

- Defining the list of target nodes whose revisions will be deleted
- Deleting a number of revisions
- Updating the current state of the batch operation

Let's see each of these steps one by one in the source code of the function:

1. Setting up the list of target nodes whose revisions will be deleted.

```
/**
 * Callback to delete revisions using Batch API.
 */
function node_revision_delete_batch_process($content_type,
  $max_revisions, &$context) {
  if (!isset($context['sandbox']['nids'])) {
    // Set initial values.
    $context['sandbox']['nids'] =
      node_revision_delete_candidates($content_type,
      $max_revisions);
    $context['sandbox']['current'] = 0;
    $context['sandbox']['total'] =
      count($context['sandbox']['nids']);
  }
```

In the preceding snippet, the `$context['sandbox']` array is being used to store the current progress of the batch operation plus the list of `nids`, which have revisions to be deleted. Take into account that the `node_revision_delete_batch_process` callback function will be called as many times as needed until the `$context['finished']` flag is set to 1. You are free to use the `$context['sandbox']` array any way you want in order to implement the logic that decides when the batch job is completed. Let's move on to step two.

2. Deleting a number of revisions.

```
// Perform the actual revision deletion.
$nid = $context['sandbox']['nids'][$context
  ['sandbox']['current']];
$deleted_revisions = _node_revision_delete_
  do_delete($nid, $max_revisions);

// Evaluate if we are done with the current node.
```

```
if (empty($deleted_revisions->pending)) {
    $context['sandbox']['current']++;
}
```

The preceding piece of code deletes a few revisions and then updates numbers within the $sandbox array. The $context['sandbox'] ['current'] array is used to determine the current node that we are pruning. Now, we will see how we evaluate whether the job has completed.

3. Updating the current state of the batch operation.

   The last part of the process callback starts by gathering some details that will be used to report how many revisions for each node ID were deleted:

   ```
   // Save some details for the final report.
   if (isset($context['results'][$nid])) {
       $context['results'][$nid] += $deleted_revisions->count;
   }
   else {
       $context['results'][$nid] = $deleted_revisions->count;
   }
   ```

Finally, the status of the batch operation is updated. As we mentioned before, if $context['finished'] equals to 1, then the batch operation is completed successfully. If it is not completed, $context['finished'] will contain the progress in a scale from 0 to 1. What we are doing in the following code is dividing the amount of processed nodes with the total amount of nodes to process:

```
// Inform the batch engine that we are not finished,
// and provide an estimation of the completion level we reached.
$context['finished'] = empty($context['sandbox']['nids']) ? 1 :
    $context['sandbox']['current'] / $context['sandbox']['total'];
}
```

# Running the command and verifying the output

Given a Drupal site with a few nodes and a lot of revisions, here is the sample command output that deletes the old ones. In the following output, we are just keeping the last two revisions of the Article content type. We are also using the --verbose option, as we want to see how Drush spawns new processes for each loop when deleting revisions:

```
$ drush --verbose node-revision-delete article 2
/home/juampy/.composer/vendor/drush/drush/drush.php --php=/usr/bin/php
  --php-options=' -d magic_quotes_gpc=Off -d magic_quotes_runtime=Off
```

```
    -d magic_quotes_sybase=Off'  --backend=2 --verbose
  --config=.git/../drush/drushrc.php --root=/home/juampy/projects/drupal
  --uri=http://default  batch-process 17 17 -u 0 2>&1
Command dispatch complete                                         [notice]
/home/juampy/.composer/vendor/drush/drush/drush.php --php=/usr/bin/php
  --php-options=' -d magic_quotes_gpc=Off -d magic_quotes_runtime=Off
  -d magic_quotes_sybase=Off'  --backend=2 --verbose
  --config=.git/../drush/drushrc.php --root=/home/juampy/projects/drupal
  --uri=http://default  batch-process 17 17 -u 0 2>&1
Command dispatch complete                                         [notice]
/home/juampy/.composer/vendor/drush/drush/drush.php --php=/usr/bin/php
  --php-options=' -d magic_quotes_gpc=Off -d magic_quotes_runtime=Off
  -d magic_quotes_sybase=Off'  --backend=2 --verbose
  --config=.git/../drush/drushrc.php --root=/home/juampy/projects/drupal
  --uri=http://default  batch-process 17 17 -u 0 2>&1
...
...

Deleted 49 revisions for node with nid 307.                      [status]
Deleted 44 revisions for node with nid 305.                      [status]
Deleted 39 revisions for node with nid 311.                      [status]
Deleted 38 revisions for node with nid 306.                      [status]
Deleted 32 revisions for node with nid 309.                      [status]
Deleted 29 revisions for node with nid 312.                      [status]
...

Command dispatch complete                                        [notice]
```

What we see in the preceding code is that Drush is spawning a new process to continue executing the task as it is not completed. It does so by invoking a command called `batch-process`. It stays on this loop until it's finally completed.

On a Drupal project with hundreds or thousands of revisions, the task will take a long time to complete, but it won't fail as it does the processing in small pieces of work. If you ever need to face a task where the amount of data to process is huge, consider making use of this approach.

# Evaluating code on the fly and running scripts

Sometimes, you need to test a piece of code after Drupal has bootstrapped, but you do not know how. I remember, when I started using Drupal, that I would copy `index.php` in `test.php`, replace the last line with whatever code I wanted to test, and then open this file in the web browser to see its result. This was an easy approach, but I felt it was wrong because I was hijacking Drupal's router: `index.php`.

Drush has two commands to let you run code after Drupal has been bootstrapped. This accomplishes the same goal as the approach mentioned in the preceding code (copying and hijacking `index.php`), but in a cleaner way. These commands are:

- `php-eval`: This lets you run PHP code in the command-line interface. It is useful when you want to test a few statements. This is like using the PHP's interactive shell (`http://php.net/manual/en/features.commandline.interactive.php`), but in a Drupal context.

- `php-script`: This executes a given script file after Drupal has been bootstrapped. It is ideal to run small snippets of code.

## The php-eval command

The `php-eval` command evaluates the given argument after bootstrapping Drupal, using the PHP's `eval()` function (`http://php.net/manual/en/function.eval.php`). It can format the output of the script in plain text plus other formats such as JSON or YAML. This comes in handy whenever you need to test a particular API or want to pipe the output of a PHP statement into something else as part of a larger script. Let's see some examples that illustrate this:

Print the title of node with `nid` as `314`:

```
$ drush php-eval 'return node_load(314)->title;'
'This is the title of node 314'
```

You can enter several statements by separating them with semicolons:

```
$ drush php-eval '$node=node_load(314); return $node->title;'
'This is the title of node 314'
```

It is best to wrap the PHP statements with single quotes because using double quotes will result in the command-line interface evaluating the string:

```
$ echo $HOME
```

```
/home/juampy
```

```
$ drush php-eval "return file_unmanaged_copy('$HOME/Pictures/image.jpg',
'public://image.jpg');"
```

```
'public://image.jpg'
```

In the preceding command, the $HOME variable is being replaced by its value (/home/juampy). Knowing this subtle difference will save you time and headaches when using this command. For example, see the error that Drush reports back when we run one of the following statements wrapped in double quotes:

```
$ drush php-eval "$node=node_load(314); return $node->title;"
```

```
PHP Parse error:  syntax error, unexpected '=' in /home/juampy/.composer/
vendor/drush/drush/commands/core/core.drush.inc(1074) : eval()'d code on
line 1
```

The preceding command throws a PHP error because the command-line interface interprets the string wrapped in double quotes attempting to replace $node with its value, which turns into an empty string when passed to the Drush command. Using single quotes, we can prevent a string that contains a $ symbol from being treated as a variable and being expanded by the shell before execution.

Finally, you can use the --format option if you want to transform the output for later processing. In the following command, we will load a node and return its data as a JSON structure:

```
$ drush php-eval --format=json 'return node_load(316);'
{
  "nid": "316",
  "uid": "1",
  "title": "Sample node",
  "log": "",
  "status": "1",
  ...
  "body": {
    "und": [
      {
        "value": "Body of the node.",
        "summary": "",
        "format": "filtered_html",
```

```
          "safe_value": "Body of the node.",
          "safe_summary": ""
        }
      ]
    },
    ...
  }
```

# The php-script command

The `php-eval` command is very useful for quickly testing one or two PHP statements, but there will be times where you need to run a few lines of code. As I discovered the `php-eval` command, I find myself using it more and more. If you ever need to check out how a certain Drupal API works or want to browse it in a data structure (a node, for example), write a small script to test this and then run it with the `php-eval` command.

Let's see this in action with a practical example. Consider that we have added an `Image` field to our `Page` content type. Then, when we are about to work with the field data, we realize that we do not know its structure. Here is a little script that will let us discover it:

```php
<?php
/**
 * @file
 * Prints the contents of the image field of a node.
 *
 * Usage: drush php-script image_field.php
 */

$node = node_load(315);
print_r($node->field_image);
```

After saving the preceding snippet at the root of our Drupal project, we can run it with the following command:

```
$ drush php-script image_field.php
Array (
  [und] => Array (
    [0] => Array (
      [fid] => 1
      [uid] => 1
```

```
            [filename] => face.jpg
            [uri] => public://face.jpg
            [filemime] => image/jpeg
            [filesize] => 49324
            [status] => 1
            [timestamp] => 1409675594
            [rdf_mapping] => Array ()
            [alt] =>
            [title] =>
            [width] => 376
            [height] => 503
        )
    )
)
```

Easy, isn't it? All of Drupal's APIs are available for this script as Drush has bootstrapped our Drupal project right before running it.

## A script to create nodes and revisions

Here is a longer example. Previously in this chapter, we reviewed how Node Revision Delete uses the Batch API to delete the older revisions of content. Before actually running the command, we needed to create some nodes with a lot of revisions otherwise the Drush command wouldn't have found anything to delete. Here is the script that we used in order to create such context prior to run drush --verbose node-revision-delete article 2:

```php
<?php
/**
 * @file
 * Script to create a bunch of nodes with revisions.
 *
 * Usage: drush php-script create_revisions.php
 */

$nodes_to_create = 10;
while ($nodes_to_create > 0) {
  // Minimum default values. We enable revisions with 'revision'
    => 1.
  $values = array(
    'type' => 'article',
```

```
  'uid' => 1,
  'status' => 1,
  'revision' => 1,
);
// Create the node entity and then use a wrapper to work with
  it.
$entity = entity_create('node', $values);
$node_wrapper = entity_metadata_wrapper('node', $entity);

// Set a random title and save the node.
$node_wrapper->title->set('Node title ' . rand(1, 100));
$node_wrapper->save();

// Create revisions for this node by simply re-saving the node a
  few times.
$revisions = rand(20, 50);
while ($revisions > 0) {
  $node_wrapper->save();
  $revisions--;
}
$nodes_to_create--;
}
```

We ran the preceding script by entering `drush php-script create_revisions. php`, which prepared the test content that we needed in order to delete old revisions with `Node Revision Delete`. This is another example of how writing small scripts and running them with Drush can be very useful in your day-to-day development.

The `php-script` and `php-eval` commands are two great tools to have in your belt. Both of them are very useful to debug logic in an isolated environment and to actually run code that does not necessarily need to be reused within a Drupal project.

# Logging messages in Drush

Writing log entries helps in spotting flaws as you read the logs to find out where a bug might be. How much we should log messages and prepare to catch errors depends on the nature of the task. A good approach is that the more critical the task, the more logging and error checking it should do. However, overly verbose logging would make our logfiles huge and hard to read. It's better if we log just the minimum needed notices, and all the errors and warnings found.

Drush uses the `drush_log()` function. This function accepts different logging levels. Here are some of them:

- `success`: This marks a successful message
- `error`: This reports an error message
- `warning`: This is used to alert about something unexpected
- `info`: This is used to print additional information

Each of the preceding list has synonyms. For example, instead of `success`, you can also use `ok`, `completed`, or `status`. In order to keep things simple, we will just use the preceding levels in the following examples. Let's see how each of them behave, given the following script:

```php
<?php
/**
 * @file logging.php
 * Sample script to test drush_log().
 */

drush_log('success: marks a successful message.', 'success');
drush_log('error: reports an error message.', 'error');
drush_log('warning: is used to alert about something.',
  'warning');
drush_log('info: is used to print additional information.',
  'info');
```

Here is the output when we run it in the command-line interface:

```
$ drush php-script logging.php
success: marks a successful message.                    [success]
error: reports an error message.                        [error]
warning: is used to alert about something.              [warning]
```

We can see that each message is printed along with its type, which is wrapped with straight brackets. If your command-line interface supports colors, `[success]` would be in green (yay!), `[error]` would be in red (ugh!), and `[warning]` would be printed in yellow (oops!). Here is something to ask ourselves though, why did the `[info]` statement not show up? We will see this in the following section.

 Drush supports Drupal's `watchdog()` function by converting it into a `drush_log()` call. This is just for compatibility purposes so that Drupal code can be executed by Drush. When writing Drush commands, always use `drush_log()`.

It is best practice to use dt() to wrap strings when logging or printing messages in order to support translations and placeholder replacement. However, the examples in the book don't use it, so they are easier to read.

# The verbose and quiet modes

By default, Drush will only print warnings and errors on the screen. There are two options which can change this behavior:

- **Drush, running in the verbose mode** (--verbose): This will print bootstrap information and all types of log entries
- **Drush, running in the quiet mode** (--quiet): This will only print warnings and errors

Hence, running Drush in the verbose mode will add [info] messages to the output:

```
$ drush --verbose php-script logging.php
success: marks a successful message.                    [success]
error: reports an error message.                          [error]
warning: is used to alert about something.              [warning]
info: is used to print additional information.             [info]
Command dispatch complete                               [notice]
```

There you are! Now, our [info] entry is shown in the output plus an extra [notice] message added by Drush itself was printed. Now, let's verify what happens if we run Drush in the quiet mode. We should see just errors and alerts:

```
$ drush --quiet php-script logging.php
error: reports an error message.                          [error]
warning: is used to alert about something.              [warning]
```

There is some reasoning in the conditional behavior of drush_log(). It is intended to give you flexibility to decide what should be logged. Drupal's cron is a great example. According to the documentation at drush topics docs-cron, this is the recommended way to run cron (some options have been removed for clarity):

```
$ /usr/local/drush/drush --root=/path/to/drupal \
--uri=mysite.example.com --quiet cron
```

In the preceding command, Drupal's cron was executed in the quiet mode. Why would we want that? The reason is that some scheduling systems (such as crontab) will send an e-mail alert if the job that got executed returned any output. The quiet mode skips the `[success]` messages, leaving just `[alerts]` and `[warnings]`. This is very useful because it will avoid us getting an e-mail every time cron runs. Instead, with the quiet mode, we will only be notified by e-mail if there was something unexpected in the process logged as a warning or as an error.

# Redirecting Drush output into a file

Some Drush commands will take time to complete and generate a long output. In such cases, it is useful to record the output into a logfile. After running a migration script, for example, you would like to thoroughly read the log, so you can check whether each migration step is completed as expected. As for cron runs, you would like to keep a log of them so that when you receive an alert, you can look at the log of the last cron runs to debug it.

Now, before you decide to redirect the output of a command into a log, you should be aware of the nature of input and output streams (http://en.wikipedia.org/wiki/Standard_streams). Each process (Drush executing a command, for example), will have three streams:

- STDIN: This is the standard input stream used to receive data (when you request the user to choose a topic out of a list using the `drush topic` command).

- STDOUT: This is the standard output stream used to print back results. If you are running a command in the command-line interface, the screen would be the one receiving this data and printing it for you.

- STDERR: This is the standard error stream used to log errors. If you are running a command and viewing its results, messages logged to STDERR will be printed on the screen, but you can choose to print them somewhere else. We will see some examples of this.

The `drush_log()` function prints messages to STDERR. If you run a Drush command, messages logged with `drush_log()` will appear on the screen once the command is completed. However, when redirecting the output of a command into a file, you should be explicit about exactly what you want to log, or you risk not logging everything you want. Let's see an example that outlines this, given the following script that we will run with Drush:

```php
<?php
/**
 * @file iostreams.php
```

```
* Sample script to test I/O streams.
*/

drush_log('Success message using drush_log()', 'success');
drush_print('Message using drush_print()');
print 'Simply printing a message with PHP\'s print function';
```

Here is the output when we execute it with Drush; redirect the output into a logfile named `iostreams.log`, and then print the contents of the resulting file:

```
$ drush php-script iostreams.php > iostreams.log
Success message using drush_log()                          [success]
$ cat iostreams.log
Message using drush_print()
Simply printing a message with PHP's print function
```

Now, this is interesting. The message that logged using `drush_log()` was printed on screen as it was written to STDERR, while the other two were saved to `iostreams.log` as both `drush_print()` and `print` write messages to STDOUT. This, most probably, is not what you want. We would prefer everything to be logged into our logfile (or if not everything, warnings, errors, and useful information). We need to be specific if we want both STDERR and STDOUT streams to be piped into a file. Here is how this can be achieved:

```
$ drush php-script iostreams.php &> iostreams.log
$ cat iostreams.log
Success message using drush_log()                          [success]
Message using drush_print()
Simply printing a message with PHP's print function
```

Depending on your needs, you might want to log both STDOUT and STDERR or just one of them. You can find great examples on how to redirect output into a file at `http://tldp.org/HOWTO/Bash-Prog-Intro-HOWTO-3.html`.

There is a nice article on why there is a different stream to log errors and how it works. If you are curious to dig further, you can visit `http://www.jstorimer.com/blogs/workingwithcode/7766119-when-to-use-stderr-instead-of-stdout`. Furthermore, PHP defines constants for each of the available streams. Visit `http://php.net/manual/en/features.commandline.io-streams.php` for more information.

# Implementing your own logging mechanism

The `drush_log()` function uses an internal function to format and print messages called `_drush_print_log()`. By looking at Drush's source code, we can see that this function is obtained through a Drush context called DRUSH_LOG_CALLBACK. Here is an excerpt of the function taken from Drush's source code:

```
// /home/juampy/.composer/vendor/drush/drush/includes/drush.inc
function drush_log($message, $type = 'notice', $error = null) {
  $log =& drush_get_context('DRUSH_LOG', array());
  $callback = drush_get_context('DRUSH_LOG_CALLBACK',
    '_drush_print_log');
  $entry = array(
    'type' => $type,
    'message' => $message,
    'timestamp' => microtime(TRUE),
    'memory' => memory_get_usage(),
  );
  $entry['error'] = $error;
  $log[] = $entry;
  drush_backend_packet('log', $entry);
  return $callback($entry);
}
```

In the preceding function, Drush uses a context variable to obtain the function name that is used to write the log message. By overriding this context variable, we would be able to implement our own function. Let's take a simple example that implements a logging function that prints to STDOUT whatever we log with `drush_log()`:

```
<?php
/**
 * @file custom_logging.php
 * Sample script to test drush_log().
 */

/**
 * Prints all log messages to STDOUT.
 *
 * @param
 *   The associative array for the entry.
 *
 * @return
 *   TRUE in all cases.
 */
```

```
function mycustom_log($entry) {
  $message = '[' . $entry['type'] . '] ' . $entry['message'];
  return drush_print($message, 0, STDOUT);
}

// Overrides Drush default's logging callback.
drush_set_context('DRUSH_LOG_CALLBACK', 'mycustom_log');

// Logs some messages to test the new setting.
drush_log('Success message using drush_log()', 'success');
drush_print('Message using drush_print()');
print 'Simply printing a message with PHP\'s print function';
```

Now, let's run the preceding code and simply redirect the STDOUT stream into a file; then, print the contents of the resulting file:

```
$ drush php-script custom_logging.php > custom_logging.log
$ cat custom_logging.log
[success] Success message using drush_log()
Message using drush_print()
Simply printing a message with PHP's print function
[debug] Returned from hook drush_core_php_script
[notice] Command dispatch complete
[memory] Peak memory usage was 8.63 MB
```

We can see that our context override statement worked like a charm; we got all log messages printed to STDOUT including the one using drush_log(). We also saw that Drush itself logged some extra messages while shutting down using drush_log() and these got logged here too. If you want to apply this to an entire Drupal project (warning! this would need thorough testing), you could add the following snippet at sites/all/drush/customlog.drush.inc:

```php
<?php
/**
 * Custom callback to log messages.
 *
 * @see _drush_print_log()
 */
function mycustom_log($entry) {
  $message = '[' . $entry['type'] . '] ' . $entry['message'];
  return drush_print($message, 0, STDOUT);
}

/**
```

```
 * Implements hook_drush_init().
 *
 * Overrides Drush's callback to write log messages.
 */
function customlog_drush_init() {
  drush_set_context('DRUSH_LOG_CALLBACK', 'mycustom_log');
}
```

With the preceding code in place, every time our code or Drush itself uses `drush_log()`, it would go through our custom logging callback.

If you just want to see messages in real time on the screen, then use `drush_print()`, which prints messages immediately to STDOUT.

# Running a command in the background

Imagine the following scenario: a new release is ready to go into the production environment. It contains changes for how articles are indexed into Apache Solr. The team has decided that once the new release has been deployed into production, you will log in to it via SSH and run a couple of Drush commands to mark the `Article` content type to be reindexed and to run the Drush command to reindex content so that all articles are submitted again to Apache Solr. This process, on large databases with a lot of content, might take a few hours to complete. If the SSH connection breaks or if we close it, the process would be killed automatically. Therefore, we should instruct it to run in the background.

Here is an example where we access the production environment and run the command in the noninteractive mode; so, even though we close the SSH connection, it would still run and save the output into a log that we can read once it finishes:

```
$ ssh produser@www.example.com
  Welcome to the Production environment!
(Production) $ cd /var/www/exampleproject/docroot
(Production) $ drush solr-mark-all article
Marked content for reindexing
(Production) $ nohup drush --verbose solr-index \
  --uri=www.example.com &> /tmp/solr_reindex.log &
[1] 12804
```

The preceding command returned to us the **process identifier (PID)** of the background process that is running our command (`12804`). It uses a few functions that you might have not seen before. These include the following:

- `nohup`: This is used to run a command that will ignore hangup signals. A hangup signal is the one sent by a process to all its subprocesses if it closes. This is what avoids the process to be killed when we close the SSH connection with the production environment.

- `&> /tmp/solr_reindex.log`: We have seen in the previous section that if we want to ensure that messages printed to STDOUT and STDERR get saved in a logfile, we need to redirect the output using `&>`. This is what we are doing here.

- `&`: This is the ampersand symbol at the end. This is used to run the command as a subprocess in the background. This lets us trigger the command and allows us to keep interacting with the command-line interface to monitor its progress or simply exit to close the SSH connection.

So, our process is running on its own now. If we list all running processes and filter them out by the keyword `solr`, we can see it listed here:

```
(Production) $ ps -aux | grep solr
produser 12804  6.0  0.8 331708 71548 pts/12    S    15:42   0:02 /usr/
bin/php -d
  magic_quotes_gpc=Off -d magic_quotes_runtime=Off -d magic_quotes_
sybase=Off
  /usr/share/drush/drush.php --php=/usr/bin/php --php-options= -d magic_
quotes_gpc=Off
  -d magic_quotes_runtime=Off -d magic_quotes_sybase=Off solr-index
  --uri=www.example.com
```

Note that the two first things listed are the user who triggered the process (`produser`) and the process identifier or PID (`12804`), while the last bit is the actual Drush command. Now, if we view the logfile interactively with the `tail` command, we can see that the process is redirecting the output of the command here as expected:

```
$ tail -f /tmp/solr_reindex.log
Indexing node 15674.                                          [ok]
Indexing node 15675.                                          [ok]
WD Apache Solr: Adding 200 documents.                     [notice]
WD Apache Solr: Indexing succeeded on 200 documents         [info]
Inspected 200 of 41045 entities. Submitted 200
```

```
    documents to Solr                                                [ok]
Indexing node 15676.                                                 [ok]
Indexing node 15677.                                                 [ok]
...
Indexing node 15678.                                                 [ok]
Indexing node 15878.                                                 [ok]
WD Apache Solr: Adding 200 documents.                            [notice]
WD Apache Solr: Indexing succeeded on 200 documents    [info]
Inspected 400 of 41045 entities. Submitted 400
    documents to Solr                                                [ok]
Indexing node 15879.                                                 [ok]
...
```

Now, we can close the SSH connection and come back later and check whether the process was completed. If for any reason we would need to terminate the process, we can do it with the kill command plus the PID:

```
(master)$ kill 12804
[1]+  Terminated  nohup drush solr-index --uri=www.example.com &>
/tmp/solr_reindex.log
```

# Summary

Running tasks in a Drupal project becomes more and more important as the project matures and scales. Things like monitoring, cleaning up and upgrading our project need to be performed in a way that the task won't stress the system too much so that Drupal doesn't crash.

Drupal's cron is a very easy and convenient mechanism to run periodic tasks. We explained how to make Drupal not fire cron when serving regular web traffic and then we moved this responsibility to Drush plus a scheduling system: Jenkins. In the next section, we saw how to decouple a particular task from cron so that it runs as an independent process. Long tasks can use the Batch API in order to split the workload into smaller chunks that can complete safely.

We closed the chapter with a few tips on how to log a command's output into a file, such as the different output modes that Drush offers (verbose or quiet).

In the next chapter, we will dive even deeper into how Drush runs commands by adding error handing and discovering a few debugging tools.

# 4
# Error Handling and Debugging

Up to this point in the book, we have covered many topics about running code with Drush. The next step is to make sure that our code runs smoothly by ensuring that input data is correct and by implementing error handling. We will also see a few tools to help us understand Drush's bootstrap even further.

In this chapter, we will cover the following topics to meet the preceding goals:

- Validating input
- Rolling back on errors
- Browsing Drush's available hooks
- Monitoring Drush's bootstrap process
- Inspecting Drupal's hooks and function implementations

## Validating input

Drush can validate input arguments before handing them over to the command's callback. In this section, we will see how to process arguments and options in order to make sure that the command's callback (the function that actually does the processing of a command) receives the right input data.

# Validating an argument

By default, Drush won't require any input arguments to execute a command, not even when you define them in the command callback. We can see this in the following example, which defines a command that expects one argument named $argument_1. We have placed this file at sites/all/drush/testcommand.drush.inc in our sample Drupal project:

```php
<?php
/**
 * @file
 * Sample Drush command to test arguments.
 */


/**
 * Implements hook_drush_command().
 */
function testcommand_drush_command() {
  $items = array();

  $items['testcommand'] = array(
    'description' => "Tests Drush command arguments",
    'arguments' => array(
      'argument_1' => 'This is a sample argument.',
    ),
  );

  return $items;
}


/**
 * Implements drush_hook_COMMAND().
 */
function drush_testcommand($argument_1) {
  var_dump($argument_1);
}
```

We have defined a command called testcommand. Now, let's execute it without arguments:

```
$ drush testcommand
Missing argument 1 for drush_testcommand()
  testcommand.drush.inc:26                                   [warning]
NULL
```

Drush logged a warning that came from PHP regarding an undefined variable expected by our command's callback, which we did not enter. As a consequence, when we printed the value of $argument_1, we got a NULL value. As you can see, Drush did not do any validation. If we want it to, we have to be explicit by adding the 'required-arguments' => TRUE option at the command definition (testcommand_drush_command()). Here is our command definition after we add it:

```
$items['testcommand'] = array(
  'description' => 'Tests Drush command arguments',
  'arguments' => array(
    'argument_1' => 'This is a sample argument.',
  ),
  'required-arguments' => TRUE,
);
```

Here is the output when we run our command again without any input arguments:

```
$ drush testcommand
Missing required argument: 'argument_1'.  See
`drush help testcommand` for information on usage.          [error]
```

Thanks to the required-arguments setting, Drush now forces us to enter a value for the required argument $argument_1. If our command expects more than one argument and only some of them are required, the required-arguments setting can also be set to a number, which defines the minimum amount of arguments that the command expects. Here is an updated version of our sample command, where the first and second arguments are required and the third one is optional:

```
/**
 * Implements hook_drush_command().
 */
function testcommand_drush_command() {
  $items = array();

  $items['testcommand'] = array(
    'description' => 'Tests Drush command arguments',
    'arguments' => array(
      'argument_1' => 'This is a sample argument.',
      'argument_2' => 'This is a sample argument.',
      'argument_3' => 'This is a sample argument.',
    ),
    'required-arguments' => 2,
  );

  return $items;
```

```
    }

    /**
     * Implements drush_hook_COMMAND().
     */
    function drush_testcommand($argument_1, $argument_2, $argument_3 =
        NULL) {
        var_dump(array($argument_1, $argument_2, $argument_3));
    }
```

Our command callback signature matches with the `required-arguments` setting: the first two arguments are required and the third one is optional (hence, it defaults to NULL). Now, we will test it with different input arguments to see how it behaves. First, we will run it with no arguments and then with just one argument:

```
$ drush testcommand
Missing required arguments: 'argument_1, argument_2'.
See `drush help testcommand` for information on usage.          [error]
$ drush testcommand one
Missing required arguments: 'argument_1, argument_2'.
See `drush help testcommand` for information on usage.          [error]
```

We can see in the preceding command executions that we must provide at least two arguments to our command or else Drush will fail to process it. Now, we will run the command with two and then three arguments, which will pass validation and then print the values:

```
$ drush testcommand one two
array(3) {
  [0] => string(1) "one"
  [1] => string(1) "two"
  [2] => NULL
}
$ drush testcommand one two three
array(3) {
  [0] => string(3) "one"
  [1] => string(3) "two"
  [2] => string(5) "three"
}
```

As we expected, validation is successful and our command prints the input values.

# Validating options

Drush has a stricter behavior for options than for arguments. It will evaluate all given options and if any of them is not supported by Drush core or the command being executed, it will throw an error. Here is an example:

```
$ drush version --foo
Unknown option: --foo.  See `drush help version` for
available options. To suppress this error, add the
option --strict=0.                                    [error]
```

As we can see in the error message, this validation can be disabled by appending the `--strict=0` option to the command invocation:

```
$ drush --strict=0 version --foo
 Drush Version   :   7.0.0-alpha5
```

When defining a command, there are two settings that alter how Drush processes its options. These are mentioned in the following sections.

# Ignoring options after the command name

The `strict-option-handling` command can be set to TRUE at the command definition when we want to allow extra options that are not known by Drush. Drush uses this setting for the `core-rsync` command, which accepts custom options for the `rsync` command that gets executed in the background to perform a recursive directory copy. Here is a simplified version of the `core-rsync` command definition:

```
$items['core-rsync'] = array(
  'description' => 'Rsync the Drupal tree to/from another server using
ssh.',
  'arguments' => array(
    'source' => 'May be rsync path or site alias. See rsync
documentation and example.aliases.drushrc.php.',
    'destination' => 'May be rsync path or site alias. See rsync
documentation and example.aliases.drushrc.php.',
  ),
  'options' => array(
    ...
    '{rsync-option-name}' => "Replace {rsync-option-name} with the
rsync option (or option='value') that you would like to pass through to
rsync.",
  ),
```

```
    'strict-option-handling' => TRUE,
  );
```

The `core-rsync` command definition accepts `rsync` specific options and uses `strict-option-handling`. Here is a sample command invocation with some options for Drush and others that are to be passed to `rsync`:

```
$ drush --yes core-rsync -v -az --exclude-paths='.git:.svn' local-files/
@site:%files
```

We mentioned in *Chapter 1*, *Introduction, Installation, and Basic Usage*, that you can place options either before or after the command name as Drush will evaluate them all. When `strict-option-handling` is set, all the options placed before the command name are processed by Drush, while options placed after the command are processed by the command. In the preceding example, `-v -az --exclude-paths='.git:.svn'` are all options that will be passed to the `rsync` command.

The `core-rsync` command calls `drush_get_original_cli_args_and_options()` in order to obtain the list of options provided in the command line and pass them to `rsync`. If you ever need to build a wrapper for a system command and want to accept its options, this function will come in handy.

## Allowing additional options

The `allow-additional-options` setting can be used at the command definition and depending on whether it is a TRUE value or an array, it means different things for Drush.

If `allow-additional-options` equals TRUE, then Drush won't validate options at all. This setting is used, for example, by the `help` command to give you the freedom to copy and paste any command after `drush help`, no matter which arguments and options it has. It will simply extract the command name and print back its full description:

```
$ drush help core-status --full --foo --bar
Provides a birds-eye view of the current Drupal installation, if any.


Examples:
 drush core-status version      Show all status lines that
contain version information.
 ...
```

Alternatively, `allow-additional-options` might contain an array of command names whose options will be supported too. This is useful when your command calls other commands using `drush_invoke()` and needs to support its options as well. For example, `sql-cli` is a Drush command that opens an interactive connection with the database. Internally, it calls the `sql-connect` command in order to build a connection string. Here, we can see the definition of `sql-cli` taken from Drush core:

```
$items['sql-cli'] = array(

   'description' => "Open a SQL command-line interface using Drupal's
credentials.",

   'bootstrap' => DRUSH_BOOTSTRAP_DRUSH,

   'allow-additional-options' => array('sql-connect'),

   'aliases' => array('sqlc'),

   'examples' => array(

      'drush sql-cli' => "Open a SQL command-line interface using
Drupal's credentials.",

      'drush sql-cli --extra=-A' => "Open a SQL CLI and skip reading
table information.",

   ),

   'remote-tty' => TRUE,

);
```

The `sql-cli` command supports the options defined by the `sql-connect` command thanks to `allow-additional-options' => array('sql-connect')`. This is why, in the `examples` section, there is an example where it uses the `--extra` option. This approach is way more flexible than manually defining the `--extra` option because if `sql-connect` adds further options in the future, we won't need to make any changes in the command definition of `sql-cli` to support them.

# Adding custom validation to a command

If we need to make custom validation of our input parameters, then it is time to implement `drush_hook_COMMAND_validate()`. This hook gets executed right before a command's callback. We will now add this hook to the contributed module: `Node Revision Delete`, which we worked with in previous chapters. Let's first see how the command works:

```
$ cd /home/juampy/projects/drupal

$ drush help node-revision-delete

Deletes old node revisions for a given content type.

Examples:
```

```
drush nrd article 50        Keeps the latest 50 revisions of every
                            article. Deletes the rest.
Arguments:
 type                       A content type's machine name.
 revisions                  The maximum amount of revisions
                            to keep per node for this content type.
Aliases: nrd
```

The `node-revision-delete` command accepts two arguments: a content type name and a number of revisions to keep for each node. These two arguments are set to be required through the `'required-arguments' => TRUE` option, but we are not checking whether the content type exists or if the amount of revisions is a positive integer. Here is our validate hook that does so:

```
// sites/all/modules/contrib/node_revision_delete/
  node_revision_delete.drush.inc
/**
 * Implements drush_hook_COMMAND_validate().
 */
function drush_node_revision_delete_validate($content_type,
$revisions_to_keep) {
  // Make sure the content type exists.
  $content_types = array_keys(node_type_get_types());
  if (!in_array($content_type, $content_types)) {
    drush_set_error('NODE_REVISION_DELETE_WRONG_TYPE', dt('The
      content type "!type" does not exist. Available content types
      are !types', array(
      '!type' => $content_type,
      '!types' => implode(', ', $content_types),
    )));
  }

  // Make sure the number of revisions is a positive integer.
  if (!is_numeric($revisions_to_keep) ||
      intval($revisions_to_keep) != $revisions_to_keep ||
      $revisions_to_keep <= 0) {
    drush_set_error('NODE_REVISION_DELETE_WRONG_REVISIONS',
      dt('The amount of revisions to keep must be a positive
      integer.'));
  }
}
```

Our `drush_node_revision_delete_validate()` validate hook takes the command arguments as input variables. Drush takes care of capturing input arguments from the command line and setting them into these two variables (`$content_type` and `$revisions_to_keep`). If the validate function returns `FALSE` or `drush_set_error()` is called, Drush won't execute the command.

The `drush_set_error()` function accepts three arguments:

- A machine name version of the error; this is useful when you want to classify errors and reuse error messages
- An optional error message to be printed to `STDERR`
- An optional label to add before the error message

Let's test our validation callback now:

```
$ drush node-revision-delete basic_page 1.5
The content type "basic_page" does not exist. Available
content types are article, feed, feed_item, page          [error]
The amount of revisions to keep must be a positive
integer.                                                   [error]
```

There we are. Our validation callback calls `drush_set_error()` as we did not enter valid arguments, which writes to `STDERR` and makes Drush stop processing the command and trigger the rollback mechanism, which we will explain in the following section.

 You can find additional documentation about error codes at `drush topic docs-errorcodes`.

# Rolling back when an error happens

When `drush_set_error()` is called during a command execution, the rollback mechanism jumps into action. The rollback mechanism gives us a chance to exit gracefully if something goes wrong. It is especially useful when we only want to perform a final action if a command is completed successfully. Drush itself uses the rollback mechanism when dealing with core and module upgrades, performing actions such as restoring original files back in place, and deleting the downloaded files of the new version if there is an error.

Here is the full sequence of invocations for a given command. In the following list, hook is the filename where the Drush command is implemented (excluding the .drush.inc extension) and COMMAND is the actual command name:

```
# 1.  hook_drush_init()
# 2.  drush_COMMAND_init()
# 3.  drush_hook_COMMAND_pre_validate()
# 4.  drush_hook_COMMAND_validate()
# 5.  drush_hook_pre_COMMAND()
# 6.  drush_hook_COMMAND()
# 7.  drush_hook_post_COMMAND()
# 8.  hook_drush_exit()
```

Also, here is the list of rollback functions that Drush will attempt to call if there is an error. Notice that it goes in backward order as the preceding list:

```
# 1.  drush_hook_post_COMMAND_rollback()
# 2.  drush_hook_COMMAND_rollback()
# 3.  drush_hook_pre_COMMAND_rollback()
# 4.  drush_hook_COMMAND_validate_rollback()
# 5.  drush_hook_COMMAND_pre_validate_rollback()
```

If there is an error, Drush will stop the execution and attempt to call rollback functions for every hook that was executed. For example, if an error happens at drush_hook_pre_COMMAND(), then Drush will call drush_hook_pre_COMMAND_rollback(), drush_hook_COMMAND_validate_rollback(), and drush_hook_COMMAND_pre_validate_rollback(). You can find plenty of documentation about these hooks at drush topic docs-api.

# Turning the update path into a single command

In order to see a practical example, we will retake the update path script that we covered in *Chapter 2, Keeping Database Configuration and Code Together*. The update path was a Bash script that called a few Drush commands in order to keep the configuration in the database in sync with the exported configuration in code. Here it is:

```
# 1. Registry Rebuild.
drush --verbose registry-rebuild --no-cache-clear
# 2. Run database updates.
drush --verbose --yes updatedb
```

```
# 3. Clear the Drush cache.
# Sometimes Features may need this due to a bug in Features module.
drush cache-clear drush
# 4. Revert all features.
drush --verbose --yes features-revert-all
# 5. Clear all caches.
drush --verbose cache-clear all
```

What we will do now is to work on a new iteration for the preceding piece of logic. We will implement the following features:

- We will wrap these commands within a custom Drush command (a Drush command can call other commands).

- We will implement drush_hook_pre_COMMAND() and drush_hook_post_ COMMAND() in order to enable and disable Drupal's maintenance mode, respectively, as a measure of precaution when we update the database.

- If something goes wrong during our command, drush_hook_post_ COMMAND() won't be invoked and instead drush_hook_COMMAND_rollback() will do, so our site will stay in maintenance mode. This is ideal as we do not want to show visitors a broken site. We will simply log an alert in the rollback callback for the administrator to take action.

Here is our update path command that we will implement within our sample Drupal project at sites/all/drush/updatepath.drush.inc. We will now explain it hook by hook. The first thing at the top of the file is the command definition:

```php
<?php
/**
 * @file
 * Drush implementation of the update path.
 */

/**
 * Implements hook_drush_command().
 */
function updatepath_drush_command() {
  $items = array();
  $items['updatepath'] = array(
    'description' => 'Runs the update path in the current site
      performing tasks such as database update, reverting
      features, etc.',
```

```
  );
  return $items;
}
```

Next, we will implement `drush_hook_pre_command()`, where we will enable Drupal's maintenance mode and kill user sessions in order to make sure that Drupal won't accept web requests when the update path command runs:

```
/**
 * Implements drush_hook_pre_command().
 */
function drush_updatepath_pre_updatepath() {
  drush_log('Enabling maintenance mode and killing active
    sessions.', 'status');
  variable_set('maintenance_mode', 1);
  db_query('truncate table {sessions}');
}
```

Now, we will actually implement each of the steps of our update path. We are making extensive use of `drush_invoke_process()` here, which is a Drush function that runs commands as subprocesses. Ideally, we should evaluate the result of these invocations in order to stop the executions if there are errors, but for simplicity, we will skip this check for now:

```
/**
 * Implements drush_hook_command().
 */
function drush_updatepath() {
  drush_invoke_process('@self', 'registry-rebuild', array(), array(
    'no-cache-clear' => TRUE,
  ));
  drush_invoke_process('@self', 'updatedb', array(), array('yes'
    => true));
  drush_invoke_process('@self', 'cc', array('type' => 'drush'));
  drush_invoke_process('@self', 'features-revert-all', array(),
    array(
    'yes' => true,
  ));
  drush_invoke_process('@self', 'cc', array('type' => 'all'));
}
```

The `@self` argument is a Drush site alias. It is used to reference a Drupal project and is covered in detail in *Chapter 5, Managing Local and Remote Environments*.

If everything goes well with the previous callbacks, then `drush_hook_post_command()` will be invoked. Here, we are implementing it in order to disable the maintenance mode and logging a message to inform that the site is not in maintenance mode anymore:

```
/**
 * Implements drush_hook_post_command().
 */
function drush_updatepath_post_updatepath() {
  drush_log('Disabling maintenance mode.', 'status');
  variable_del('maintenance_mode');
}
```

Alternatively, if there was an error during our command, our site will stay in maintenance mode because `drush_hook_post_command()` won't be invoked, but `drush_hook_command_rollback()` will. We are implementing this hook in the following code just to alert that maintenance mode is still on:

```
/**
 * Implements drush_hook_command_rollback().
 */
function drush_updatepath_rollback() {
  drush_log('Oh no! Something went wrong. Review the above log and
    disable maintenance mode when done.', 'error');
}
```

Let's run `drush updatepath` in our sample Drupal project and verify its output. Note that we are using the `--verbose` options to see `[status]` messages. The following output is a simplified version for clarity:

```
$ cd /home/juampy/projects/drupal
$ drush --verbose updatepath
Enabling maintenance mode and killing active sessions.         [status]
The registry has been rebuilt via registry_rebuild (A).        [success]
The Drupal caches have NOT been cleared after all
  registry rebuilds.                                           [warning]
It is highly recommended you clear the Drupal caches as
  soon as possible.                                            [warning]
All registry rebuilds have been completed.                     [success]
No database updates required                                   [success]
'all' cache was cleared.                                       [success]
Finished performing updates.                                        [ok]
```

```
'drush' cache was cleared.                                    [success]

Current state already matches defaults, aborting.                  [ok]

'all' cache was cleared.                                      [success]

Disabling maintenance mode.                                   [success]
```

We can see that the first and last messages of the preceding output are our `pre` and `post` command hooks. There is also a warning from the `Registry Rebuild` module telling us to clear caches as soon as possible, which we do right after we run database updates. This was a smooth run. Now, let's suppose that there is an error. The last message, instead of being `Disabling maintenance mode.` `[success]`, would be the following one:

```
Oh no! Something went wrong. Review the above log and
    disable maintenance mode when done.                         [error]
```

The preceding message is called due to Drush's rollback mechanism. We are simply alerting that the maintenance mode is still active. If you need to take action when a command fails, then the rollback mechanism is the place to do it.

# Browsing hook implementations

So far, we saw some hooks that Drush supports before and after running a command. In order to discover them, Drush offers a debugging mode to view all the hooks that we can implement for a given command and check whether they were executed or not on runtime.

In the following example, we will define a very simple command that we will use to test the handy option `--show-invoke`, which prints all the function callbacks where Drush attempts to find a match. We will create this command under `$HOME/.drush/testhooks.drush.inc`, which makes it available for us everywhere in the command-line interface for our user:

```php
<?php
/**
 * @file
 * Sample Drush command to test hook invocations.
 */

/**
 * Implements hook_drush_command().
 */
function testhooks_drush_command() {
```

```
    $items = array();
    $items['testhooks'] = array(
       'description' => 'Dummy command to test command invocations.',
        // No bootstrap at all.
       'bootstrap' => DRUSH_BOOTSTRAP_DRUSH,
    );
    return $items;
}


/**
 * Implements drush_hook_COMMAND().
 */
function drush_testhooks() {
    // Leaving it empty. Just want to see what happens before and
      after.
}
```

Now that we have our sample command, which Drush hooks do we have available? How should we name them after? Let's run the command with the --show-invoke option to see them:

```
$ cd /home/juampy
$ drush --show-invoke testhooks
Available drush_invoke() hooks for testhooks:                      [ok]
drush_testhooks_pre_validate
drush_archive_testhooks_pre_validate
drush_browse_testhooks_pre_validate
...
drush_testhooks_validate
drush_archive_testhooks_validate
drush_browse_testhooks_validate
...
drush_testhooks_pre_testhooks
drush_archive_pre_testhooks
drush_browse_pre_testhooks
...
drush_testhooks [* Defined in /home/juampy/.drush/testhooks.drush.inc]
drush_archive_testhooks
drush_browse_testhooks
...
```

```
drush_testhooks_post_testhooks
drush_archive_post_testhooks
drush_browse_post_testhooks
...
```

```
Available rollback hooks for testhooks:                               [ok]
drush_testhooks_rollback
```

Drush first checks whether each hook has been implemented at `testhooks.drush.inc` and then looks at all the command files in core and the following locations (see `drush topic docs-commands` for further details):

- Drush's core commands directory. For example, `/home/juampy/.composer/vendor/drush/drush/commands`.

- Directories added manually through the `--include` option, such as `drush --include=/home/juampy/projects/drupal/sites/all/drush testhooks`.

- The system-wide shared directory. For example, `/usr/share/drush/commands`.

- The `.drush` folder in our home directory, which is where we implemented our `testhooks` command in the preceding section

- The `/drush` and `/sites/all/drush` directories within the current Drupal installation.

- All the enabled modules in the current Drupal installation.

Now, let's change directory into our sample Drupal project and run it again. Notice that we defined our command at `testhooks_drush_command()` to use `'bootstrap'` => `DRUSH_BOOTSTRAP_DRUSH`, which means that we don't want to bootstrap Drupal at all:

```
$ cd /home/juampy/projects/drupal
$ drush --show-invoke testhooks
Available drush_invoke() hooks for testhooks:                         [ok]
drush_testhooks_pre_validate
drush_archive_testhooks_pre_validate
drush_browse_testhooks_pre_validate
drush_registry_rebuild_testhooks_pre_validate
drush_testcommand_testhooks_pre_validate
drush_updatepath_testhooks_pre_validate
...
```

Drush did not look for command implementations at Drupal project's installed modules as our command does not need it. For commands that do not need to bootstrap a Drupal site, this is a performance boost as Drush does not spend time doing it before running our command. However, if your command might benefit from having a Drupal project bootstrapped, then you can set the bootstrap setting to DRUSH_BOOTSTRAP_MAX, which attempts to bootstrap a Drupal project if it is available. We will now update our command definition at /home/juampy/.drush/ testhooks.drush.inc and then run it again within our Drupal project to verify that it now looks into the installed modules for command hook implementations. Here is the command with the bootstrap setting changed:

```
/**
 * Implements hook_drush_command().
 */
function testhooks_drush_command() {
  $items = array();
  $items['testhooks'] = array(
    'description' => 'Dummy command to test command invocations.',
    // No bootstrap at all.
    'bootstrap' => DRUSH_BOOTSTRAP_MAX,
  );
  return $items;
}
```

Here is the output when we run the command:

```
$ cd /home/juampy/projects/drupal
$ drush --show-invoke testhooks
Available drush_invoke() hooks for testhooks:        [ok]
drush_testhooks_pre_validate
drush_archive_testhooks_pre_validate
drush_browse_testhooks_pre_validate
drush_ctools_testhooks_pre_validate
drush_features_testhooks_pre_validate
drush_newsfetcher_testhooks_pre_validate
```

There you are! Now, Drush is also looking for command hook implementations at contributed (`ctools`, `features`) and custom modules (`newsfetcher`) in our Drupal project. If we implement any of these functions, they will be called by Drush. We will dive even deeper into Drush's bootstrap phases in the following section.

# Inspecting the bootstrapping process

When Drush is called, it goes over a set of bootstrap steps that are very similar to how Drupal bootstraps on a web request. Drush commands might require minimum bootstrap phase to run. Here is a simplified list of each of Drush's bootstrap steps based on the documentation at `drush topic docs-bootstrap`:

1. DRUSH_BOOTSTRAP_DRUSH: This is the minimum bootstrap phase. It just loads Drush configuration and core files.

2. DRUSH_BOOTSTRAP_DRUPAL_ROOT: This checks whether there is a valid Drupal's root directory available. It is useful for commands that deal with a whole Drupal installation and not a specific site at the `sites` directory.

3. DRUSH_BOOTSTRAP_DRUPAL_SITE: This will load Drush's configuration of a specific site within the `sites` directory of a Drupal project, but it won't load `settings.php`.

4. DRUSH_BOOTSTRAP_DRUPAL_CONFIGURATION: This loads the site's `settings. php` file.

5. DRUSH_BOOTSTRAP_DRUPAL_DATABASE: This connects to the site's database, so database queries against a Drupal project can be made from this phase onwards.

6. DRUSH_BOOTSTRAP_DRUPAL_FULL: This loads all the available APIs in the Drupal project.

7. DRUSH_BOOTSTRAP_DRUPAL_LOGIN: This logs in as a given user defined by the `--user` option. The default value is to use the anonymous user.

8. DRUSH_BOOTSTRAP_MAX: This will try to bootstrap Drupal as far as possible, but it does not require a Drupal project to be available.

The default phase, if none is set, when defining a command at `hook_drush_command()` is DRUSH_BOOTSTRAP_DRUPAL_LOGIN. We used the last one (DRUSH_BOOTSTRAP_MAX) at our `testhooks` custom command in order to execute it both with and without the context of a Drupal project.

Drush's `--debug` option can also provide useful information regarding how far Drush reached in the bootstrap process. Here is a sample command output:

```
$ cd /home/juampy/projects/drupal
$ drush --debug testhooks
```

We started by changing the directory into our Drupal project and then ran our sample command with the `--debug` option to see how the bootstrap process works. Here is the output step by step:

```
Drush bootstrap phase : _drush_bootstrap_drush()           [bootstrap]
Loading drushrc "/home/juampy/.drush/drushrc.php" into
  "home.drush" scope.                                      [bootstrap]
Loading drushrc
  "sites/all/drush/drushrc.php" into "drupal" scope.       [bootstrap]
```

Step 1 (DRUSH_BOOTSTRAP_DRUSH) is completed. Drush has been bootstrapped and it has loaded all the configuration files that it found available: one at the `.drush` directory under our home path and the other at the current Drupal project where we are. Let's move on to step 2:

```
Drush bootstrap phase :
  _drush_bootstrap_drupal_root()                           [bootstrap]
Initialized Drupal 7.29-dev root directory at
  /home/juampy/projects/drupal                             [notice]
```

The DRUSH_BOOTSTRAP_DRUPAL_ROOT phase is completed. We now know that we are within a Drupal project and can access its root directory with `drush_get_context('DRUSH_DRUPAL_ROOT')` from our command if we need to. Let's move on to the next phase:

```
Drush bootstrap phase :
  _drush_bootstrap_drupal_site()                           [bootstrap]
Initialized Drupal site default at sites/default           [notice]
```

The DRUSH_BOOTSTRAP_DRUPAL_SITE phase is completed. We can now gain access to the directory of the selected site under the sites directory with `drush_get_context('DRUSH_SELECTED_DRUPAL_SITE_CONF_PATH')`. Here is the output for the next phase:

```
Drush bootstrap phase :
  _drush_bootstrap_drupal_configuration()                  [bootstrap]
```

The DRUSH_BOOTSTRAP_DRUPAL_CONFIGURATION phase has completed loading the settings.php file located at sites/default within our Drupal project. Let's move on to the next step:

```
Drush bootstrap phase :
  _drush_bootstrap_drupal_database()                        [bootstrap]
Successfully connected to the Drupal database.              [bootstrap]
```

The DRUSH_BOOTSTRAP_DRUPAL_DATABASE phase is completed and now we can query the database in our command using Drupal's database APIs:

```
Drush bootstrap phase :
  _drush_bootstrap_drupal_full()                            [bootstrap]
```

In DRUSH_BOOTSTRAP_DRUPAL_FULL, all of the available APIs in our Drupal project are loaded and our command can make use of them if needed:

```
Drush bootstrap phase :
  _drush_bootstrap_drupal_login()                           [bootstrap]
Successfully logged into Drupal as  (uid=0)                 [bootstrap]
```

We did not provide a user with the --user option when we ran our command, so Drush used the special user with uid as 0 (the anonymous user) on the DRUSH_BOOTSTRAP_DRUPAL_LOGIN phase. If you need a specific user to run a command (for example, when your code is creating content), consider adding the --user option to your command with the user ID that you need:

```
Found command: testhooks (commandfile=testhooks)           [bootstrap]
Calling hook drush_testhooks                                   [debug]
Returned from hook drush_testhooks                            [debug]
Command dispatch complete                                     [notice]
 Timer  Cum (sec)  Count  Avg (msec)
 page    0.308       1       308.06
Peak memory usage was 26.38 MB                               [memory]
```

Our command was executed and Drush finished the process. Note that there was no log entry for DRUSH_BOOTSTRAP_MAX as this is not a phase, but an order for Drush to bootstrap as far as possible.

# Inspecting hook and function implementations

The Devel module (https://www.drupal.org/project/devel) has a couple of commands that are extremely useful when either looking for hook implementations or locating functions within a Drupal installation. We will see them in action in the following sections.

# Browsing and navigating hook implementations

The fn-hook command lists all modules implementing a given hook name. This command comes in very handy when you want to implement a hook, but want to check before whether any other modules implement it and what do they do.

Let's take hook_cron() as an example. In *Chapter 3, Running and Monitoring Tasks in Drupal Projects*, we spoke about the importance of extracting some tasks out of hook_cron() and moved them into a custom Drush command so that they could run on their own process and scheduling. Let's go to our sample Drupal project and run the command to see which modules implement hook_cron(). We will assume that the Devel module is already downloaded and installed:

```
$ cd /home/juampy/projects/drupal
$ drush fn-hook cron
Enter the number of the hook implementation you wish to view.
  [0]   :  Cancel
  [1]   :  ctools
  [2]   :  dblog
  [3]   :  feeds
  [4]   :  field
  [5]   :  job_scheduler
  [6]   :  node
  [7]   :  node_revision_delete
  [8]   :  search
  [9]   :  system
  [10]  :  update
```

We can see in the preceding output that the `fn-hook` command lists all modules implementing `hook_cron()` sorted by module weight and filename, so you can get an idea of the order in which these callbacks will be executed. The output is listed as a select list where each module has an option number; Drush waits for us to enter a value in the command line. We will choose option 3 (the `Feeds` module) and hit *Enter*:

```
3
// file: /home/juampy/projects/drupal/sites/all/modules/contrib/feeds/
feeds.module, lines 48-63
/**
 * Implements hook_cron().
 */
function feeds_cron() {
  if ($importers = feeds_reschedule()) {
    foreach ($importers as $id) {
      feeds_importer($id)->schedule();
      $rows = db_query("SELECT feed_nid FROM {feeds_source} WHERE id =
:id", array(':id' => $id));
      foreach ($rows as $row) {
        feeds_source($id, $row->feed_nid)->schedule();
      }
    }
    feeds_reschedule(FALSE);
  }
  // Expire old log entries.
  db_delete('feeds_log')
    ->condition('request_time', REQUEST_TIME - 604800, '<')
    ->execute();
}
```

Drush printed the `Feed` module's `hook_cron()` implementation, plus a heading with its file location and start and end lines. How cool is that?

# Viewing source code of a function or method

The second handy command that comes with the Devel module to quickly view a particular piece of code is fn-view. It is specially helpful when you remember a function name, but not where it is defined. This command accepts a function or class method and prints its contents and location, if found. Here is an example where we print the contents of the drupal_debug() function, a debugging function provided by the Devel module that prints a variable into a temporary logfile:

```
$ drush fn-view drupal_debug
// file: /home/juampy/projects/drupal/sites/all/modules/contrib/devel/
devel.module, lines 1788-1797
/**
 * Logs a variable to a drupal_debug.txt in the site's temp directory.
 *
 * @param mixed $data
 *   The variable to log to the drupal_debug.txt log file.
 * @param string $label
 *   (optional) If set, a label to output before $data in the log file.
 *
 * @return void|false
 *   Empty if successful, FALSE if the log file could not be written.
 *
 * @see dd()
 * @see http://drupal.org/node/314112
 */
function drupal_debug($data, $label = NULL) {
  $out = ($label ? $label . ': ' : '') . print_r($data, TRUE) . "\n";

  // The temp directory does vary across multiple simpletest instances.
  $file = file_directory_temp() . '/drupal_debug.txt';
  if (file_put_contents($file, $out, FILE_APPEND) === FALSE) {
    drupal_set_message(t('Devel was unable to write to %file.',
array('%file' => $file)), 'error');
    return FALSE;
  }
}
```

We can also view class methods with `fn-view`. Here, we are viewing the contents of the `render()` method of the `views_handler_field` class, which is the base class to define custom fields in the `Views` module:

```
$ drush fn-view views_handler_field::render
// file: /home/juampy/projects/drupal/sites/all/modules/contrib/views/
handlers/views_handler_field.inc, lines 1021-1024
  function render($values) {
    $value = $this->get_value($values);
    return $this->sanitize_value($value);
  }
```

These two methods are very useful to inspect code quickly. Keep in mind that both of them have their limitations: `fn-hook` cannot list all the available hooks in a Drupal project and instead expects you to provide the hook to search for, while `fn-view` can only print functions that are loaded by Drupal automatically either by the `.info` or `.module` files.

# Summary

In this chapter, we covered many tools to help you write safe code and make the most of Drush's APIs. We started by discovering how input data is processed by Drush and how we can alter its behavior to fit our needs. Custom validation can also be implemented in a hook so that it runs its checks before the actual command.

Preparing our commands for unexpected errors is key in any project. Drush's rollback mechanism gives us a chance to take action if a command fails, so we can make any required cleanup and logging. We saw how our update path script can benefit from this mechanism in order to become more robust.

For times when we are writing a custom command, being aware of which Drush hooks are available and when they are executed is useful in order to split the logic in the most appropriate way. The `--show-invoke` option provides detailed information about each of the callbacks that Drush attempts to call during a command execution.

Whenever we use a command, Drush goes through a bootstrap process in a way that mimics Drupal's bootstrap. Understanding each of the different phases is vital in order to decide which APIs are available for a given command's callback. We saw that we can inspect Drush's bootstrap process on the fly with the `--debug` option.

Finally, we wrapped up the chapter with some usage examples of the Devel module's `fn-hook` and `fn-view` commands, which can be helpful to navigate through hook implementations and functions.

In the next chapter, we will discover one of the killer features of Drush: managing local and remote sites using site aliases.

# 5
# Managing Local and Remote Environments

I remember the first time I used a Drush site alias. Someone in the team mentioned them and after reading the documentation, I set up one for the production environment. Then, to test it, I entered `drush @prod.example.com core-status`. Drush silently logged in to the production server, ran the command, and printed the result back to my screen. It was a revelation. Until then, running Drush commands in the production environment involved:

- Opening a remote session with the production environment
- Changing directory to the root of the Drupal project
- Running Drush commands
- Closing the remote session

The fact of being able to run Drush commands for the production environment from my local environment was mind-blowing. A stream of ideas came to my head: I would be able to check module versions, run a small piece of code to test something, download the database and files, and so on. All my respects to the Drush team (especially to Greg Anderson) for creating site aliases.

In this chapter, we will see how Drush site aliases can be configured to manage the different environments of a Drupal project. Here are the topics that we will cover:

- Managing local environments
- Managing remote environments
- Special site aliases
- Running the update path in remote sites
- Copying database and files between environments

# Managing local environments

Drush site aliases offer a useful way to manage local environments without having to be within Drupal's root directory.

A site alias consists of an array of settings for Drush to access a Drupal project. They can be defined in different locations, using various file structures. You can find all of its variations at `drush topic docs-aliases`. In this chapter, we will use the following variations:

- We will define local site aliases at `$HOME/.drush/aliases.drushrc.php`, which are accessible anywhere for our command-line user.
- We will define a group of site aliases to manage the development and production environments of our sample Drupal project. These will be defined at `sites/all/drush/example.aliases.drushrc.php`.

In the following example, we will use the `site-alias` command to generate a site alias definition for our sample Drupal project:

```
$ cd /home/juampy/projects/example
$ drush --uri=example.local site-alias --alias-name=example.local @self
$aliases["example.local"] = array (
  'root' => '/home/juampy/projects/example',
  'uri' => 'example.local',
  '#name' => 'self',
);
```

The preceding command printed an array structure for the `$aliases` variable. You can see the `root` and `uri` options here, which we saw in previous chapters when we needed to tell Drush about the location of our Drupal project. There is also an internal property called `#name` that we can ignore. Now, we will place the preceding output at `$HOME/.drush/aliases.drushrc.php` so that we can invoke Drush commands to our local Drupal project from anywhere in the command-line interface:

```
<?php

/**
 * @file
 * User-wide site alias definitions.
 *
 * Site aliases defined here are available everywhere for the current
 user.
```

```
  */

  // Sample Drupal project.
  $aliases["example.local"] = array (
    'root' => '/home/juampy/projects/example',
    'uri' => 'example.local',
  );
```

Here is how we use this site alias in a command. The following example is running the `core-status` command for our sample Drupal project:

```
$ cd /home/juampy
$ drush @example.local core-status
 Drupal version              :  7.29-dev
 Site URI                    :  example.local
 Database driver             :  mysql
 Database username           :  root
 Database name               :  drupal7x
 Database                    :  Connected
 ...
 Drush alias files           :  /home/juampy/.drush/aliases.drushrc.
php
 Drupal root                 :  /home/juampy/projects/example
 Site path                   :  sites/default
 File directory path         :  sites/default/files
```

Drush loaded our site alias file and used the `root` and `uri` options defined in it to find and bootstrap Drupal. The preceding command is equivalent to the following one, which we saw in previous chapters:

```
$ drush --root=/home/juampy/projects/example \
  --uri=example.local core-status
```

While `$HOME/.drush/aliases.drushrc.php` is a good place to define site aliases in your local environment, `/etc/drush` is a first class directory to place site aliases in servers. Let's discover now how we can connect to remote environments via Drush.

# Managing remote environments

Site aliases that reference remote websites can be accessed by Drush through a password-less SSH connection (http://en.wikipedia.org/wiki/Secure_Shell). Before we start with these, let's make sure that we meet the requirements.

# Verifying requirements

First, it is recommended to install the same version of Drush in all the servers that host your website. Drush will fail to run a command if it is not installed in the remote machine except for `core-rsync`, which runs `rsync`, a non-Drush command that is available in Unix-like systems.

If you can already access the server that hosts your Drupal project through a public key, then skip to the next section. If not, you can either use the `pushkey` command from Drush extras (https://www.drupal.org/project/drush_extras), or continue reading to set it up manually.

# Accessing a remote server through a public key

The first thing that we need to do is generate a public key for our command-line user in our local machine. Open the command-line interface and execute the following command. We will explain the output step by step:

```
$ cd $HOME
$ ssh-keygen
Generating public/private rsa key pair.
Enter file in which to save the key (/home/juampy/.ssh/id_rsa):
```

By default, SSH keys are created at `$HOME/.ssh/`. It is fine to go ahead with the suggested path in the preceding prompt; so, let's hit *Enter* and continue:

```
Created directory '/home/juampy/.ssh'.
Enter passphrase (empty for no passphrase): *********
Enter same passphrase again: *********
```

If the `.ssh` directory does not exist for the current user, the `ssh-keygen` command will create it with the correct permissions. We are next prompted to enter a passphrase. It is highly recommended to set one as it makes our private key safer. Here is the rest of the output once we have entered a passphrase:

```
Your identification has been saved in /home/juampy/.ssh/id_rsa.
Your public key has been saved in /home/juampy/.ssh/id_rsa.pub.
```

```
The key fingerprint is:
6g:bf:3j:a2:00:03:a6:00:e1:43:56:7a:a0:c7:e9:f3 juampy@juampy-box
The key's randomart image is:
+--[ RSA 2048]----+
|                 |
|                 |
|..               |
|o..*             |
|o + . . S        |
| + * = . .       |
|   = O o . .     |
|   *.o * . .     |
|    .oE oo.      |
+-----------------+
```

The result is a new hidden directory under our $HOME path named .ssh. This directory contains a private key file (id_rsa) and a public key file (id_rsa.pub). The former is to be kept secret by us, while the latter is the one we will copy into remote servers where we want to gain access.

Now that we have a public key, we will announce it to the SSH agent so that it can be used without having to enter the passphrase every time:

```
$ ssh-add ~/.ssh/id_rsa
Identity added: /home/juampy/.ssh/id_rsa (/home/juampy/.ssh/id_rsa)
```

Our key is ready to be used. Assuming that we know an SSH username and password to access the server that hosts the development environment of our website, we will now copy our public key into it. In the following command, replace exampledev and dev.example.com with the username and server's URL of your server:

```
$ ssh-copy-id exampledev@dev.example.com
exampledev@dev.example.com's password:
Now try logging into the machine, with "ssh
'exampledev@dev.example.com'", and check
in: ~/.ssh/authorized_keys to make sure we
haven't added extra keys that you weren't
expecting.
```

Our public key has been copied to the server and now we do not need to enter a password to identify ourselves anymore when we log in to it. We could have logged on to the server ourselves and manually copied the key, but the benefit of using the `ssh-copy-id` command is that it takes care of setting the right permissions to the `~/.ssh/authorized_keys` file. Let's test it by logging in to the server:

```
$ ssh exampledev@dev.example.com

Welcome!
```

We are ready to set up remote site aliases and run commands using the credentials that we have just configured. We will do this in the next section.

If you have any trouble setting up SSH authentication, you can find plenty of debugging tips at `https://help.github.com/articles/generating-ssh-keys` and `http://git-scm.com/book/en/Git-on-the-Server-Generating-Your-SSH-Public-Key`.

# Defining a group of remote site aliases for our project

Before diving into the specifics of how to define a Drush site alias, let's assume the following scenario: you are part of a development team working on a project that has two environments, each one located in its own server:

- Development, which holds the bleeding edge version of the project's codebase. It can be reached at `http://dev.example.com`.

- Production, which holds the latest stable release and real data. It can be reached at `http://www.example.com`.

- Additionally, there might be a variable amount of local environments for each developer in their working machines; although, these do not need a site alias.

Given the preceding scenario and assuming that we have SSH access to the development and production servers, we will create a group of site aliases that identify them. We will define this group at `sites/all/drush/example.aliases.drushrc.php` within our Drupal project:

```php
<?php
/**
 * @file
 *
 * Site alias definitions for Example project.
```

```
  */

// Development environment.
$aliases['dev'] = array(
  'root' => '/var/www/exampledev/docroot',
  'uri' => 'dev.example.com',
  'remote-host' => 'dev.example.com',
  'remote-user' => 'exampledev',
 );

// Production environment.
$aliases['prod'] = array(
  'root' => '/var/www/exampleprod/docroot',
  'uri' => 'www.example.com',
  'remote-host' => 'prod.example.com',
  'remote-user' => 'exampleprod',
 );
```

The preceding file defines two arrays for the `$aliases` variable keyed by the environment name. Drush will find this group of site aliases when being invoked from the root of our Drupal project. There are many more settings available, which you can find by reading the contents of the `drush topic docs-aliases` command.

These site aliases contain options known to us: `root` and `uri` refer to the remote root path and the hostname of the remote Drupal project. There are also two new settings: `remote-host` and `remote-uri`. The former defines the URL of the server hosting the website, while the latter is the user to authenticate Drush when connecting via SSH.

Now that we have a group of Drush site aliases to work with, the following section will cover some examples using them.

# Using site aliases in commands

Site aliases prepend a command name for Drush to bootstrap the site and then run the command there. Our site aliases are `@example.dev` and `@example.prod`. The word `example` comes from the filename `example.aliases.drushrc.php`, while `dev` and `prod` are the two keys that we added to the `$aliases` array. Let's see them in action with a few command examples:

*Check the status of the Development environment*:

```
$ cd /home/juampy/projects/example
$ drush @example.dev status
 Drupal version            :   7.26
 Site URI                  :   http://dev.example.com
 Database driver           :   mysql
 Database username         :   exampledev
 Drush temp directory      :   /tmp
 ...
 Drush alias files         :
   /home/juampy/projects/example/sites/all/drush/example.aliases.drushrc.
php
 Drupal root               :   /var/www/exampledev/docroot
 ...
```

The preceding output shows the current status of our development environment. Drush sent the command via SSH to our development environment and rendered back the resulting output. Most Drush commands support site aliases. Let's see the next example.

*Log in to the development environment and copy all the files from the files directory located at the production environment*:

```
$ drush @example.dev site-ssh
   Welcome to example.dev server!
$ cd `drush @example.dev drupal-directory`
$ drush core-rsync @example.prod:%files @self:%files
You will destroy data from /var/www/exampledev/docroot/sites/default/
files and replace with data from exampleprod@prod.example.com:/var/www/
exampleprod/docroot/sites/default/files/

Do you really want to continue? (y/n): y
```

Note the use of @self in the preceding command, which is a special Drush site alias that represents the current Drupal project where we are located. We are using @self instead of @example.dev because we are already logged inside the development environment. Now, we will move on to the next example.

*Open a connection with the Development environment's database:*

```
$ drush @example.dev sql-cli
Welcome to the MySQL monitor.  Commands end with ; or \g.
mysql> select database();
+------------+
| database() |
+------------+
| exampledev |
+------------+
1 row in set (0.02 sec)
```

The preceding command will be identical to the following set of commands:

```
drush @example.dev site-ssh
cd /var/www/exampledev
drush sql-cli
```

However, Drush is so clever that it opens the connection for us. Isn't this neat? This is one of the commands I use most frequently. Let's finish by looking at our last example.

*Log in as the administrator user in production:*

```
$ drush @example.prod user-login
   http://www.example.com/user/reset/1/some-long-token/login
   Created new window in existing browser session.
```

The preceding command creates a login URL and attempts to open your default browser with it. I love Drush!

# Special site aliases

We defined two site aliases for our project: one for the development environment and one for the production environment. However, when we list all the available site aliases, we see a few extra ones:

```
$ cd /home/juampy/projects/example
$ drush site-alias
example
example.dev
example.local
example.prod
none
self
```

We can see that this project has six Drush site aliases. We are aware of @example.local, @example.dev, and @example.prod, but what about the others? Those are site aliases defined by Drush automatically. We will explain each of them in the following sections through examples.

# Running a command on all site aliases of a group

The example alias is a group site alias for our example project. If you prepend a command with it, the command will be executed on all the site aliases defined under this group. Our example.aliases.drushrc.php file defines two aliases: dev and prod. This can be useful for analysis tasks such as to check which version of a module each environment has. The following example checks this for the Metatag module:

```
$ cd /home/juampy/projects/example
$ drush @example pm-info --fields=version metatag
You are about to execute 'pm-info metatag' non-interactively (--yes
forced) on all of the following targets:
  @example.dev
  @example.prod
Continue?  (y/n): y
@example.dev   >>  Version   :  7.x-1.0-rc2+5-dev
@example.prod  >>  Version   :  7.x-1.0-rc2
```

As we can see from the preceding code, after prompting for a confirmation, Drush has logged in to each environment, executed the `pm-info` command, and printed back the result. We are using a slightly more recent version of the `Metatag` module at the development environment than at production. The `+5-dev` bit is a syntax used by `Drupal.org` to inform how far a development release is ahead of a given release.

# Avoiding a Drupal bootstrap with @none

The `@none` alias is another special Drush site alias. It forces Drush not to bootstrap the current Drupal project. We used it in *Chapter 2, Keeping Database Configuration and Code Together*, in order to download the `Registry Rebuild` command without bootstrapping Drupal because at that moment it was broken. Here is an example where we change directory to the root of our Drupal project and run the `core-status` command with the `@none` site alias, which will make Drush ignore the Drupal project where we are located:

```
$ cd /home/juampy/projects/example
$ drush @none status
 PHP executable        :  /usr/bin/php
 PHP configuration     :  /etc/php5/cli/php.ini
 PHP OS                :  Linux
 Drush version         :  7.0.0-alpha3
 Drush temp directory  :  /tmp
 Drush configuration   :  /home/juampy/.drush/drushrc.php
 Drush alias files     :  sites/all/drush/example.aliases.drushrc.php
```

The result of the command just refers to the Drush environment and not to the Drupal project, thanks to the use of the `@none` site alias. Drush did not go through any of the Drupal bootstrap phases.

# Referencing the current project with @self

Last but not least, `@self` is used in Drush commands that accept a site alias as an argument when we want to reference the current project where we are located. Commands that support this are, among others, `sql-sync` and `core-rsync`. Here is an example where we install a copy of the development environment's database into our local environment:

```
$ drush sql-sync @example.dev @self
You will destroy data in example and replace with data from server.
juampy.com/drupaldev.
```

```
Do you really want to continue? (y/n): y
Starting to dump database on Source.                           [ok]
Copying dump file from Source to Destination.                  [ok]
Starting to import dump file onto Destination database.        [ok]
```

In the preceding command, `@self` is the target destination of the database dump. This means that the database dump extracted from the development environment will be copied into our local environment, which is where we are currently located in the command line.

# Adding site alias support to the update path

In *Chapter 2*, *Keeping Database Configuration and Code Together*, we introduced the update path as a list of steps to update a database so that it gets in sync with the exported configuration in code. Then, in *Chapter 4*, *Error Handling and Debugging*, we made the update path more flexible by wrapping it in a Drush command and taking advantage of Drush's command hooks in order to perform steps before and after it runs. In this chapter, we will go one step further by implementing the following improvements:

- Make sure that the `registry-rebuild` and `features-revert-all` commands are available.

- Add an example in the command definition using a site alias.

- Implement error handling by inspecting the returned status from each command. If a command fails, we will stop the process immediately.

# Inspecting the command implementation and hooks

We will now go through our update path command, located at `sites/all/drush/updatepath.drush.inc`, explaining the new features hook by hook. The first one at the top of the file is the command definition:

```php
<?php
/**
 * @file
 * Runs a set of steps to update a database to be in line with code.
 */
```

```
/**
 * Implements hook_drush_command().
 */
function updatepath_drush_command() {
  $items = array();
  $items['updatepath'] = array(
    'description' => 'Runs the update path in the bootstrapped site
performing tasks such as database updates, reverting features, etc.',
    'drush dependencies' => array('registry_rebuild', 'features'),
    'examples' => array(
      'drush updatepath' => 'Runs the updatepath in the current Drupal
project.',
      'drush @example.dev updatepath' => 'Runs the updatepath in the
Drupal project referenced by @example.dev.',
    ),
  );
  return $items;
}
```

We have added a couple of settings to the command definition: the first one is drush
dependencies, which tells Drush to make sure that the command files registry_
rebuild.drush.inc and features.drush.inc are found or abort otherwise. The
second one is an example of how to execute the update path using a site alias. As
you can see, all you need to do is prepend the command with the site alias name
and Drush will run each of the steps of the update path in the Drupal site referenced
by the site alias. Now, we will see the command hook that gets triggered before the
command starts:

```
/**
 * Implements drush_hook_pre_command().
 */
function drush_updatepath_pre_updatepath() {
  drush_log('Enabling maintenance mode and killing active sessions.',
'status');
  $return = drush_invoke_process('@self', 'variable-set',
array('maintenance_mode', 1), array(
    'yes' => TRUE,
    'always-set' => TRUE,
  ));
```

```
  if ($return['error_status']) {
    return drush_set_error('UPDATEPATH_PRE_MAINTENANCE', 'Could not
enable maintenance mode.');
  }
  $return = drush_invoke_process('@self', 'sql-query', array('truncate
table sessions'));
  if ($return['error_status']) {
    return drush_set_error('UPDATEPATH_PRE_SESSIONS', 'Could not
truncate user sessions.');
  }
}
```

In `drush_hook_pre_command()`, we perform actions before updating the database. In this case, the actions consist of enabling maintenance mode and killing all user sessions. We have added error checks to these tasks; so if they fail, we stop the process. The next step is our actual command implementation:

```
/**
 * Implements drush_hook_command().
 */
function drush_updatepath() {
  // Registry rebuild.
  $return = drush_invoke_process('@self', 'registry-rebuild', array(),
array('no-cache-clear' => TRUE));
  if ($return['error_status']) {
    return drush_set_error('UPDATEPATH_RR', 'registry-rebuild
failed.');
  }

  // Database updates.
  $return = drush_invoke_process('@self', 'updatedb', array(),
array('yes' => true));
  if ($return['error_status']) {
    return drush_set_error('UPDATEPATH_UPDB', 'updatedb failed.');
  }

  // Clear Drush cache (sometimes needed before reverting Features
components).
  $return = drush_invoke_process('@self', 'cache-clear', array('type'
=> 'drush'));
```

```
    if ($return['error_status']) {
      return drush_set_error('UPDATEPATH_CC_DRUSH', 'cache-clear
  failed.');
    }


    // Revert all Features components.
    $return = drush_invoke_process('@self', 'features-revert-all',
  array(), array(
      'yes' => TRUE,
    ));
    if ($return['error_status']) {
      return drush_set_error('UPDATEPATH_FRA', 'features-revert-all
  failed.');
    }


    // Clear all caches.
    $return = drush_invoke_process('@self', 'cache-clear', array('type'
  => 'all'));
    if ($return['error_status']) {
      return drush_set_error('UPDATEPATH_CC_ALL', 'cache-clear
  failed.');
    }
  }
```

We have added error checks after each step. If something goes wrong, we log an error and terminate. Note that each command invocation being made with drush_ invoke_process() uses @self as the site alias. You might think that in order for this command to support Drush site aliases, it should pick up the site alias from the command line and use it. However, when using a site alias, Drush sends each of these commands to be run at the Drupal project referenced by the site alias. This means that @self would point our local Drupal project if we run drush updatepath or a remote Drupal project if we run drush @example.prod updatepath. This is the beauty of site aliases. We will now see the implementation of the post-command actions that will run if there were no errors up to this point:

```
  /**
   * Implements drush_hook_post_command().
   */
  function drush_updatepath_post_updatepath() {
    drush_log('Disabling maintenance mode.', 'success');
```

```
  $return = drush_invoke_process('@self', 'variable-delete',
array('maintenance_mode'), array(
    'yes' => TRUE,
    'exact' => TRUE,
  ));
  if ($return['error_status']) {
    return drush_set_error('UPDATEPATH_POST_MAINTENANCE', 'Could not
disable maintenance mode.');
  }
}
```

We are simply disabling maintenance mode in the preceding code and logging a message. We will now see the last section of our command file that implements rollback hooks to take action if there is an error:

```
/**
 * Implements drush_hook_command_rollback().
 */
function drush_updatepath_rollback() {
  drush_log('Oh no! Something went wrong. Review the above log and
disable maintenance mode when done.', 'error');
  drush_set_context('UPDATEPATH_ROLLBACK', TRUE);
}


/**
 * Implements drush_hook_pre_command_rollback().
 */
function drush_updatepath_pre_updatepath_rollback() {
  if (!drush_get_context('UPDATEPATH_ROLLBACK')) {
    drush_log('Oh no! Something went wrong prior to start the update
path. Check the status of the maintenance mode and the sessions
table.', 'error');
  }
}
```

We have implemented two rollback hooks: one is for the pre-command actions and the second one is for the command implementation. As you can see, we are simply logging a sensible message with tips on how to proceed if an error happens. Note the use of `drush_set_context()` and `drush_get_context()`, which is helping us to avoid getting two messages if an error happens during the command execution; one for `drush_updatepath_rollback()` and then a second one for `drush_hook_pre_command_rollback()`.

# Running the update path with a site alias

Our `updatepath` command has a built-in site alias support. We actually did not have to add anything special to it apart from using `@self` at each of the update commands.

Assuming that we have deployed the `updatepath` command into the development environment of our `example` project, let's now see the result of running it from our local environment using a site alias:

```
$ cd /home/juampy/projects/example
$ drush @example.dev updatepath
Enabling maintenance mode and killing active sessions.          [status]
maintenance_mode was set to "1".                               [success]
The registry has been rebuilt via registry_rebuild (A).        [success]
The registry has been rebuilt via
   drush_registry_rebuild_cc_all (B).                          [success]
The caches have not been cleared. It is recommended you
   clear the Drupal caches as soon as possible.                [warning]
All registry rebuilds have been completed.                     [success]
No database updates required                                   [success]
'all' cache was cleared.                                        [success]
Finished performing updates.                                        [ok]
'drush' cache was cleared.                                      [success]
Current state already matches defaults, aborting.                   [ok]
'all' cache was cleared.                                        [success]
Disabling maintenance mode.                                    [success]
maintenance_mode was deleted.                                  [success]
```

The preceding command was executed at our remote server where `http://dev.example.com` runs. Drush logged in to the server via SSH and executed the sequence of commands printing its progress in real time. If we want to run the update path on the production environment, we would do it with `drush @example.prod updatepath` or we could also do `drush @example.prod ssh` and then run it there with `drush updatepath`. Let's now see an example when an error happens. The rollback mechanism should start and our rollback hooks will be executed:

```
$ drush @example.dev updatepath
Enabling maintenance mode and killing active sessions.          [status]
maintenance_mode was set to "1".                               [success]
The registry has been rebuilt via registry_rebuild (A).        [success]
The registry has been rebuilt via
   drush_registry_rebuild_cc_all (B).                          [success]
The caches have not been cleared. It is recommended you
   clear the Drupal caches as soon as possible.               [warning]
All registry rebuilds have been completed.                    [success]
No database updates required                                   [success]
'all' cache was cleared.                                        [success]
Finished performing updates.                                        [ok]
ouch!                                                            [error]
Oh no! Something went wrong. Review the above log
   and disable maintenance mode when done.                      [error]
```

We can see that the command stopped its execution and the rollback mechanism logged as message alerting us that the maintenance mode is still active. We could now log in to the development environment with `drush @example.dev ssh` and inspect what went wrong.

# Copying database and files between environments

Now that we have our site aliases configured, we can benefit from running two of the most powerful Drush commands: `sql-sync` and `core-rsync`. The former is used to copy the database from a Drupal project to another, while the latter copies files between Drupal projects. In this section, we will see some suggestions to make them safer and efficient in our projects.

Previously in this chapter, we have seen examples of both these commands. They take two site aliases as arguments. The first one is the *from* (also known as source) and the second one is the *to* (also known as destination). I like to mentally tell it to myself when I type these commands so that I make sure that I copy them in the right direction. I mumble *drush sql-sync from to*. The reason for such thoroughness is that when running `core-rsync` and `sql-sync` commands, the order does matter a lot. Here is an example: while working in a development team, we would run these commands every once in a while to update our local environment with the latest code and database:

```
$ cd /home/juampy/projects/example
# Gets latest version of code in the current branch.
$ git pull --rebase
$ drush sql-sync @example.prod @self    # Downloads production database.
$ drush updatepath       # Syncs the database with code.
```

However, some day, we might not pay enough attention and mistype the `sql-sync` command in the following way:

```
$ drush sql-sync @self @example.prod
```

Oh no! We just copied our local database full of testing content with photos of bunnies into production.

As you can see, the flexibility and power that Drush site aliases bring to a team comes at a risk. In order to prevent the preceding catastrophe, we could do one or more of the following options:

- Only give SSH access to the production environment to a few developers, so the preceding command wouldn't work as Drush would not be able to log in to production

- Copy production's database into development every night and ask the team to sync with development instead of production

- Suggest the team to use a Drush shell alias when running `sql-sync`

- Block these commands through Drush's API when the destination is production

The first option is probably the safest, but you still need to give the rest of the team a chance to download a relatively fresh copy of the production environment so that it can test its code changes locally. The second option can be achieved with the help of a Continuous Integration tool such as Jenkins, which will be covered in *Chapter 6, Setting Up a Development Workflow*. The last two options are the ones that we will implement in this chapter.

# Defining Drush shell aliases for a team

Drush shell aliases are command shortcuts. It resembles Unix's command-line aliases, which are normally defined at $HOME/.bashrc. Here are some of the command-line aliases I have in my local environment:

```
$ alias
...
alias example='cd /home/juampy/projects/example'
alias egrep='egrep --exclude=*~ --exclude-dir=.git --exclude-dir=files'
alias chmod8='sudo setfacl -R -m u:www-data:rwX -m u:`whoami`:rwX sites/
default/files'
alias killd8='rm -rf sites/default/files && rm sites/default/settings.php
&& dr...'
...
```

Given the preceding list, if I type example in the command line, it would be the same as if I had run cd /home/juampy/projects/example. Likewise, Drush supports shell aliases in configuration files for commands that we use frequently. Drush configuration files can be placed at several places in our system for Drush to load them, and you can find the full list at drush topics docs-configuration. In our case, we will just create a Drush configuration file for our Drupal project at sites/all/drush/drushrc.php with the following aliases:

```php
<?php

/**
 * @file
 * Drush configuration for Sample project.
 */

// Shell aliases.
$options['shell-aliases']['syncdb'] = '--verbose --yes sql-sync @
example.dev @self --create-db';
$options['shell-aliases']['syncfiles'] = '--verbose --yes core-rsync @
example.dev:%files/ @self:%files/';
```

We have defined two Drush shell aliases in the preceding code: syncdb and syncfiles. Whenever we run drush syncdb or drush syncfiles, Drush will execute the command that these two wrap. Before we try them, let's make sure that Drush can load them with the shell-alias command:

```
$ cd /home/juampy/projects/example/
$ drush shell-alias
 wipe          :  cache-clear all
 unsuck        :  pm-disable -y overlay,dashboard
 offline       :  variable-set -y --always-set maintenance_mode 1
 online        :  variable-delete -y --exact maintenance_mode
 pm-clone      :  pm-download --gitusername=juampy@git.drupal.org
--package-handler=git_drupalorg
 syncdb        :  --verbose --yes sql-sync @example.dev @self --create-db
 syncfiles     :  --verbose --yes rsync @example.dev:%files/ @self:%files/
```

We can see our custom Drush shell aliases at the bottom of the list. The other ones listed are some useful shortcuts that you can find at drush topics docs-configuration. I encourage you to run drush topic docs-configuration > $HOME/.drush/drushrc.php and then adjust the resulting file as it comes with very useful settings for Drush that will be available for all your Drupal projects.

Let's now test our syncdb shell alias:

```
$ drush syncdb
Initialized Drupal 7.31 root directory at
/home/juampy/projects/example                          [notice]
You will destroy data in example and replace with data from
dev.example.com/drupaldev.
Do you really want to continue? (y/n): y
Starting to create database on Destination.            [ok]
Creating database example. Any possible existing database
will be dropped!
Do you really want to continue? (y/n): y
Starting to dump database on Source.                   [ok]
Database dump saved to /home/exampledev/drush-backups/exampledev/
201409231429/exampledev_20140923_1429.sql.gz           [success]
Starting to discover temporary files directory on
```

```
Destination.                                                 [ok]
Copying dump file from Source to Destination.                [ok]
Starting to import dump file onto Destination database.      [ok]
Command dispatch complete                               [notice]
```

The preceding output is a simplified version. The original one is longer because we used the `--verbose` option that shows how Drush bootstraps each project (local and development), generates a database dump, downloads it, and installs it. It's handy to leave the verbose option set, so if there are any errors or warnings, they can be easily spotted. Now, let's try our site alias to sync files from development into our local environment:

```
$ drush syncfiles
Initialized Drupal 7.31 root directory at
/home/juampy/projects/example                           [notice]
You will destroy data from
/home/juampy/projects/example/sites/default/files/
andreplace with data from
exampledev@dev.example.com:
   /var/www/exampledev/docroot/sites/default/files/
Do you really want to continue? (y/n): y
receiving incremental file list
...
sent 14.71M bytes  received 31 bytes  1.28M bytes/sec
total size is 16.18M  speedup is 1.10
Command dispatch complete                               [notice]
```

The preceding Drush site alias synced the `files` directory from the development environment into our local environment. As you can see, these two aliases come in handy for the rest of the team, so these do not need to deal with having to type the full syntax for `sql-sync` and `core-rsync` commands.

# Blocking the execution of certain commands

Using Drush shell aliases instead of manually typing `sql-sync` and `core-rsync` commands is definitely an improvement, but there is still the chance of someone writing the command manually in the wrong way and causing a disaster. We can go one step further in securing these commands and leverage Drush's command API to block certain commands. Drush has a section in its documentation with a few default policy rules. We will use this file as a template to make our own policy file for the `example` project:

```
$ drush topic docs-policy > sites/all/drush/policy.drush.inc
```

After editing the resulting file, we have the following policy rules for our project:

```php
<?php

/**
 * @file
 * Policy rules for Example project.
 */

/**
 * Implements drush_hook_COMMAND_validate().
 *
 * Prevent overriding Production's database.
 */
function drush_policy_sql_sync_validate($source = NULL, $destination =
NULL) {
  if ($destination == '@example.prod') {
    return drush_set_error('POLICY_DENY_SQL', dt('Oops, you almost
copied your database onto Production. Please use drush syncdb
instead.'));
  }
}

/**
 * Implements drush_hook_COMMAND_validate().
 *
```

```
 * Prevent modifying Production's files directory.
 */
function drush_policy_core_rsync_validate($source = NULL, $destination
= NULL) {
  if (strpos($destination, '@example.prod') === 0) {
    return drush_set_error('POLICY_DENY_RSYNC', dt('Oops, you almost
copied files onto Production. Please use drush syncfiles instead.'));
  }
}
```

We have implemented a validate hook for `sql-sync` and `core-rsync` commands, verifying that the destination site of the command being executed is not production and throwing an error if so. Let's try copying our local database into production and see what happens:

```
$ drush cache-clear drush
```

```
$ drush sql-sync @self @example.dev
```

You will destroy data in dev.example.com/exampledev and replace with data from example.

Do you really want to continue? (y/n): y

Oops, you almost copied your database onto Production. Please

   use drush syncdb instead.                                  [error]

As we added a new command file, we cleared Drush's cache so that it could discover it. Next, we tried to copy our database into the production environment and our policy file aborted it as we expected. Let's try now to sync our files directory into the production environment:

```
$ drush rsync @self:%files @example.dev:%files
```

@example.dev:%files

Oops, you almost copied files onto Production. Please use

   drush syncfiles instead.                                   [error]

It's the same case here. By using Drush shell aliases and implementing policy rules, you can limit some of the flexibility of Drush site aliases that can damage your project and at the same time provide shorter commands for the team to use.

# Ignoring tables on sql-sync

The `sql-sync` command accepts a list of tables whose data will be skipped and a list of tables whose data and structure will be skipped. This feature speeds up the command considerably, especially on large databases. Here is an example where we manually define the list of tables to ignore when copying development's database into our local environment:

```
$ drush sql-sync \
  --structure-tables-list=cache,history,sessions,watchdog \
    @example.dev @self
```

Now, the list of tables provided will just be created in our local database, but its data won't be downloaded from the development environment. The `--structure-tables-list` is actually an option of the `sql-dump` command, which `sql-sync` calls in order to obtain a database dump from the development environment and then download it. Managing this list of tables can be tedious as the list would be changing frequently during the development stage of a project. In order to simplify this process, we can instead use the `--structure-tables-key` option and define an array of tables at our Drush configuration file. Here is our `sites/all/drush/drushrc.php` file with the list of tables to ignore:

```php
<?php

/**
 * @file
 * Drush configuration for Sample project.
 */

/**
 * List of tables whose *data* is skipped by the 'sql-dump' and 'sql-sync'
 * commands when the "--structure-tables-key=common" option is
 * provided.
 */
$options['structure-tables']['common'] = array('cache', 'cache_*',
'history', 'search_*', 'sessions', 'watchdog');

// Shell aliases.
```

```
$options['shell-aliases']['syncdb'] = '--verbose --yes sql-sync @
example.dev @self --create-db';
$options['shell-aliases']['syncfiles'] = '--verbose --yes rsync @
example.dev:%files/ @self:%files/';
```

We have defined a list of `structure-tables` under the `common` key. This list supports wildcards, which makes it considerably shorter. Now, here is how we can reference this list when we run `sql-sync`:

**`$ drush sql-sync --structure-tables-key=common @example.dev @self`**

The preceding command will ignore the data of many more tables than the previous one, which was using `--structure-tables-list`. Drush loads our configuration file at `sites/all/drush/drushrc.php` and is able to relate the common key provided in the command line with the list of tables to ignore in the development environment. We can even go one step further and move the `--structure-tables-key` option into our development's site alias, so we do not even have to type this option anymore. Here is our site alias definition after adding the `--structure-tables-key` option at `sites/all/drush/example.aliases.drushrc.php`:

```php
<?php
/**
 * @file
 *
 * Site alias definitions for Example project.
 */

// Development environment.
$aliases['dev'] = array(
  'root' => '/var/www/exampledev',
  'uri' => 'http://dev.example.com',
  'remote-host' => 'dev.example.com',
  'remote-user' => 'exampledev',
  'command-specific' => array (
    'sql-dump' => array (
      'structure-tables-key' => 'common',
    ),
  ),
);
```

```
// Production environment.
$aliases['prod'] = array(
  'root' => '/var/www/exampleprod/docroot',
  'uri' => 'www.example.com',
  'remote-host' => 'www.example.com',
  'remote-user' => 'exampleprod',
);
```

We have added an option to the `sql-dump` command whenever `@example.dev` is used. As we said before, `sql-sync` internally calls `sql-dump` to obtain a database dump from the source site alias; hence, the option is set for `sql-dump` and not `sql-sync`. Now, we can use `sql-sync`, and Drush will silently ignore the list of tables that we defined previously:

```
$ drush sql-sync @example.dev @self
```

The preceding code will load the `--structure-tables-key` option from development's site alias and the list of tables from our Drush configuration file. Our Drush shell alias will behave in the same way so that the rest of the team can keep on using `drush syncdb` and Drush will take care of ignoring unnecessary tables.

Drush site aliases offer many more options such as `--source-command-specific` and `--target-command-specific`, which should offer enough flexibility to fit your team's needs. Take a look at `drush topic docs-aliases` for further examples that you can consider useful for your project.

# Summary

Site aliases open a world of possibilities. They are one of the gems of Drush (and perhaps Drupal as well). The community built a lot of tools that rely on them and you can discover these at `Drupal.org`.

In this chapter, we covered practical examples with site aliases. We started by defining a site alias for our local Drupal project, and then went on to write a group of site aliases to manage remote environments for a hypothetical Drupal project with a development and production site. Before using site aliases for our remote environments, we covered the basics of setting up SSH in order for Drush to connect to these servers and run commands there.

We also learned that Drush automatically defines a set of special site aliases: `@self`, `@none`, plus one for each group of site aliases that we define. The `@self` alias means *Bootstrap the current project*, `@none` means *Don't bootstrap the current project*, and a group site alias such as `@example` means *Run the command in all the sites defined within the group.*

Next, we tested a custom command with a remote site alias and took the chance to improve it, exploring Drush's APIs even further. We showed how running the update path in our local and in a remote site makes little difference to Drush. As a matter of fact, when I finished writing this chapter, I published the command in `Drupal.org`. You can find this at `https://www.drupal.org/project/updatepath` or by running `drush dl updatepath`.

We finished the chapter configuring two commands that use site aliases as arguments: `core-rsync` and `sql-sync`. The tips that we learned will help us to make these two commands easier and safer to use within a team of developers. This setup will be the foundation of our next and last chapter, where we will leverage all of Drush's features to set up a development workflow for a team.

# 6
# Setting Up a Development Workflow

A few years ago, I joined a team to work on a web development project. On the first day, I got the following e-mail from the CTO:

*Hi Juampy!*

*Welcome to the team. Here is how you can start working:*

*Clone the repository* `git@github.com:some-company/some-project.git`

*Download the database from* `http://intranet.some-company.com/some-project/db.sql.tar.gz`

*Set up your local environment and then open* `http://jira.some-company.com` *to start working on tickets.*

*Thanks and good luck!*

I hope that you can figure out how I felt when I read this e-mail. If you can't, let me tell you that the project was a chaos, there was no effort to keep a certain level of quality; there were bugs everywhere and it took me two days to reach the project's homepage in my environment. This is definitely not a good welcome for a new developer. Here is an alternative e-mail that I got in a different team:

*Hi Juampy!*

*Welcome to the project, I have just given you access to the project's repository. Please open up* `https://github.com/some-company/some-project` *and follow instructions there to get started.*

*Thanks and good luck!*

The preceding URL presented the README.md file of the project with clear steps on how to set up a local environment, how to update it, and which tools and resources I had available. This experience was way more positive than the previous e-mail we saw above. The team had a development workflow. They understood that their code travelled from their local to development environment and finally the production environment, while content would stream back in the opposite direction from production to their local environments.

Drush can help a team to standardize many of the common tasks that they encounter every day in a Drupal project. In this chapter, we will leverage Drush concepts that we studied previously to implement a development workflow for a team. Here are some of the topics that we will cover:

- Moving configuration, commands, and site aliases out of Drupal
- Configuring the development database for the team
- Running post sql-sync tasks in local environments

# Moving configuration, commands, and site aliases out of Drupal

Drupal's .htaccess file does a good job of blocking the execution of command files because their extension is drush.inc, but configuration files have a drushrc.php extension; hence, these will be executed by the web server if someone writes the full path in the browser. Let's test this in the command line. Our sample Drupal project has a few Drush commands and a configuration file at sites/all/drush:

```
$ curl -v http://example.local/sites/all/drush/policy.drush.inc
* Connected to example.local (127.0.0.1) port 80 (#0)
> GET /sites/all/drush/policy.drush.inc HTTP/1.1
> User-Agent: curl/7.35.0
> Host: example.local
> Accept: */*
>
< HTTP/1.1 403 Forbidden
```

We attempted to access our policy command file from the web browser and failed because Drupal's `.htaccess` file blocked access to it. Good! Now let's try this with our main Drush configuration file:

```
$ curl -v http://example.local/sites/all/drush/drushrc.php
* Connected to example.local (127.0.0.1) port 80 (#0)
> GET /sites/all/drush/drushrc.php HTTP/1.1
> User-Agent: curl/7.35.0
> Host: example.local
> Accept: */*
>
< HTTP/1.1 200 OK
```

Gotcha! Drupal's `.htaccess` file allowed access to `drushrc.php` so the web browser executed the code from that file. Although there is no output because `drushrc.php` simply sets a few array variables, it could be dangerous if we add further logic to it. Drush command files and configuration are not meant to be viewed in a web browser. Therefore, why have them under our project's document root? In this section, we will move all of our custom Drush configuration, commands, and site aliases one level above and then tell Drush how to find them.

# Installing Drupal Boilerplate

In order to move Drush files out of Drupal, there must be a parent directory within our codebase. We need to set up a directory structure where `docroot` will contain our Drupal project and everything else that does not need to be available to the web browser is out.

Drupal Boilerplate (`https://github.com/Lullabot/drupal-boilerplate`) is a GitHub project that we will use as a foundation to structure Drupal projects. It comes with the following file structure:

- `docroot`: This is an empty directory where we will place our example Drupal project.

- `drush`: This will host configuration, commands, and aliases for Drush.

- `patches`: This can be used to keep track of core and contrib patches.

- `results`: This stores automated test results. It is useful when you want a third-party software to parse them.

- `scripts`: These are project scripts. For example, we can store shell scripts used by Jenkins jobs here.

- `tests`: These are automated test scripts and not SimpleTest scripts, but tests implemented with other testing technologies such as CasperJS or Behat.

- `.gitignore`: These are the default set of files and patterns to be ignored by Git.

- `README.md`: This is the main project's documentation and is meant to be adjusted for your project and the starting point for everyone new to the team.

Here is how we can download Drupal Boilerplate and then place Drupal into its `docroot` directory. We start by downloading Drupal Boilerplate into our temporary directory:

```
$ cd /tmp
$ wget https://github.com/Lullabot/drupal-boilerplate/archive/master.zip
HTTP request sent, awaiting response... 200 OK
Length: 40891 (40K) [application/zip]
Saving to: 'master.zip'
100%[=====================================>] 40.891      160KB/s   in
0,2s
'master.zip' saved [40891/40891]
```

Drupal Boilerplate has been downloaded to `/tmp/master.zip`. Let's unzip its contents:

```
$ unzip master.zip
Archive:  master.zip
   creating: drupal-boilerplate-master/
  inflating: drupal-boilerplate-master/.gitignore
   creating: drupal-boilerplate-master/docroot/
  inflating: drupal-boilerplate-master/docroot/readme.md
   creating: drupal-boilerplate-master/drush/
   creating: drupal-boilerplate-master/drush/aliases/

...
```

Now, we will move our Drupal `example` project into `docroot` and then move Drupal Boilerplate to be the root of our project. Note that we are using `rsync` instead of `mv` because the latter does not move hidden files such as .htaccess:

```
$ rsync -v -a /home/juampy/projects/example/
  drupal-boilerplate-master/docroot/
sending incremental file list
./
.gitignore
.htaccess
CHANGELOG.txt
COPYRIGHT.txt
INSTALL.mysql.txt
INSTALL.pgsql.txt
INSTALL.sqlite.txt
...
sent 24,016,476 bytes  received 75,003 bytes  16,060,986.00 bytes/sec
total size is 23,692,782  speedup is 0.98


$ mv /tmp/drupal-boilerplate-master /home/juampy/projects/example
```

We need to adjust our local web server configuration, so the root of `http://example.local` points now to `/home/juampy/projects/example/docroot`. The same applies to the development and production environments. Furthermore, this directory change also affects our site alias definitions, which need to be updated. Here is what they look like after adjusting them at `docroot/sites/all/drush/drush/example.aliases.drushrc.php`:

```php
<?php
/**
 * @file
 *
 * Site alias definitions for Example project.
 */

// Development environment.
$aliases['dev'] = array(
```

```
    'root' => '/var/www/drupal-dev/docroot',
    'uri' => 'http://dev.example.com',
    'remote-host' => 'dev.example.com',
    'remote-user' => 'juampydev',
    'command-specific' => array (
      'sql-dump' => array (
        'structure-tables-key' => 'common',
      ),
    ),
  );

  // Production environment.
  $aliases['prod'] = array(
    'root' => '/var/www/exampleprod/docroot',
    'uri' => 'http://www.example.com',
    'remote-host' => 'prod.example.com',
    'remote-user' => 'exampleprod',
  );
```

We are done relocating Drupal within the new directory structure. Welcome to Drupal Boilerplate!

# Relocating Drush files

Now that we have our new directory structure in place, we can move Drush configuration, commands, and site aliases from sites/all/drush to drush. Let's take a look at the contents of this directory for our sample Drupal project:

```
$ ls docroot/sites/all/drush/
drushrc.php
example.aliases.drushrc.php
policy.drush.inc
registry_rebuild
updatepath.drush.inc
```

We have a mix of configuration files (`drushrc.php`), custom command files (`policy.drush.inc` and `updatepath.drush.inc`), site aliases files (`example.aliases.drushrc.php`), and a contributed project with a command file in it (`registry_rebuild`). We will reorganize them with the following commands:

Our Drush configuration file `drushrc.php` goes to `drush`:

**$ mv docroot/sites/all/drush/drushrc.php drush/**

Custom command files go to `drush/commands`:

**$ mv docroot/sites/all/drush/*.drush.inc drush/commands/**

Site aliases go to `drush/aliases`:

**$ mv docroot/sites/all/drush/example.aliases.drushrc.php drush/aliases/**

Let's remove `Registry Rebuild` from `docroot/sites/all/drush` because Drupal Boilerplate already has it at `drush/commands`:

**$ rm -rf docroot/sites/all/drush/registry_rebuild**

Now that we have relocated Drush files, how will they be discovered? Drush, while bootstrapping, is able to find resources at several locations in the system and the current Drupal project. On top of that, it can be provided with additional resources. We will add the following file at `docroot/sites/all/drush/drushrc.php`, which does a sanity check and then tells Drush where our configuration, commands, and site aliases are:

```php
<?php

/**
 * @file
 * Drush configuration for Sample project.
 *
 * Loads configuration files located out of the document root.
 */

// Safety check. Only run in the command line.
if (php_sapi_name() != 'cli') {
  return;
```

```
}

// Load Drush configuration, commands and site alias files from
docroot/../drush.
$drupal_dir = drush_get_context('DRUSH_SELECTED_DRUPAL_ROOT');
if ($drupal_dir) {
  include_once $drupal_dir . '/../drush/drushrc.php';
  $options['include'][] = $drupal_dir . '/../drush/commands';
  $options['alias-path'][] = $drupal_dir . '/../drush/aliases';
}
```

We have added a safety measure at the top of the file; so, if someone opens
`http://example.local/sites/all/drush/drushrc.php` in a web browser, then
no code will be executed. Next, we obtained Drupal's root directory through Drush's
context system and we used it to add configuration, commands, and aliases located
in the parent directory.

There are many ways to structure and load external configuration, commands, and
site aliases in Drush. The `drush topic docs-configuration` command suggests
a neat way of doing it through the project's Git repository. In this book, we did not
choose this strategy because Git might not be available in the development and
production environments.

# Testing the new setup

Let's test that our new Drush setup works as expected. We will now run Drush's
`core-status` command from the root of our Drupal project using the `--verbose`
option to check where the configuration is being loaded from. We will analyze the
command output as it goes:

```
$ cd /home/juampy/projects/example/docroot
$ drush --verbose core-status
Include /home/juampy/projects/example/docroot/../drush/commands
                                                              [notice]

Initialized Drupal 7.31 root directory at
/home/juampy/projects/example/docroot                         [notice]
```

Gotcha! Very early in Drush's bootstrap, our new directory containing Drush commands has been included. Let's see the next chunk of the command's output:

```
Initialized Drupal site default at sites/default            [notice]
 Drupal version    :  7.31
 Site URI                        :  http://default
 Database driver                 :  mysql
 Database hostname               :  localhost
 Database port                   :
 Drush configuration             :  /home/juampy/projects/example/
docroot/sites/all/drush/drushrc.php /home/juampy/.drush/drushrc.php
```

Drush loaded two configuration files: one from our the $HOME path (which we defined in *Chapter 5, Managing Local and Remote Environments*) and another one that is inside our project at sites/all/drush/drushrc.php. Although, we do not see drush/drushrc.php listed here, we know that it has been loaded by sites/all/drush/drushrc.php through an include_once statement. Let's inspect the rest of the command's output:

```
 Drush alias files               :  /home/juampy/.drush/aliases.drushrc.
php
/home/juampy/projects/example/docroot/../drush/aliases/example.aliases.
drushrc.php
 Drupal root                     :  /home/juampy/projects/example/docroot
 Site path                       :  sites/default
 File directory path             :  sites/default/files
 Temporary file directory path   :  /tmp


Command dispatch complete                [notice]
```

Our project's site aliases were loaded from their new location. Note the /../, which we used at sites/all/drush/drushrc.php to access the parent directory of docroot. What about our custom shell aliases, which are now defined at drush/drushrc.php? Are they being loaded? Let's list the available shell aliases to verify it:

```
$ cd /home/juampy/projects/example/docroot
$ drush shell-alias
 wipe         :  cache-clear all
 unsuck       :  pm-disable -y overlay,dashboard
 offline      :  variable-set -y --always-set maintenance_mode 1
```

```
online      :  variable-delete -y --exact maintenance_mode
pm-clone    :  pm-download --gitusername=juampy@git.drupal.org
--package-handler=git_drupalorg
syncdb      :  --verbose --yes sql-sync @example.dev @self --create-db
syncfiles   :  --verbose --yes rsync @example.dev:%files/ @self:%files/
```

That's perfect. We can still use these shell aliases to download the database and files from the development environment. We are done! We have successfully moved our Drush configuration and commands out of Drupal.

# Configuring the development database for the team

The development environment's database is the one that everyone in the team should download to work with. The production's database can be downloaded to our local environment in very specific occasions when we need bleeding edge fresh data and when we are aware of the security implications of using it.

By working with the development environment's database, we gain the following benefits:

- The development environment's database might not need tables that are present in production, such as old migration tables.

- Compromising data in the development environment can be sanitized after the database has been copied from production. Therefore, when developers download the development's database into their local environments, they get a safe database to work with.

- Large tables containing data that is not needed for development can be trimmed down, thus reducing the size of the database, which helps for faster performance of the sql-sync command.

- E-mail submission can be short circuited or forwarded to a logfile or dummy address.

In the previous chapter, we added a few adjustments to the sql-sync command for the team to download a copy of the development environment to their local environment. We will now work to fine tune the other side of the coin: the job that periodically copies the production environment's database and files into development. You can set this up in many ways: a crontab in development, a shell script in your local environment that logs in to the development environment, a Jenkins job that has SSH access to the development environment to open a connection, and so on. In this book, we will use Jenkins to set up a job that runs periodically.

# Configuring Jenkins to sync production to development

Our `example` project has two remote site aliases referencing the development and production environments. We will now add the development server as a Jenkins node and then create a job where Jenkins will log in to development and run the `sql-sync` and `core-rsync` commands.

First of all, we need to create a `jenkins` user in development and give Jenkins SSH access to it. You can find instructions to accomplish this at `http://www.caktusgroup.com/blog/2012/01/10/configuring-jenkins-slave`.

Once we have configured the `jenkins` user and SSH access, we can proceed to add the node by clicking on **New Node** at the Jenkins administration interface. We are then presented with the following screenshot:

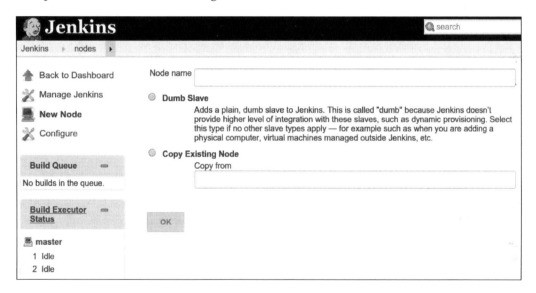

At **Node name**, we will give a name to the Jenkins node. For this case, we will type in `ExampleDev` as this node references the server that hosts `http://dev.example.com`. We will then choose **Dumb Slave** and click on **OK**. On the next page, we can configure the new node:

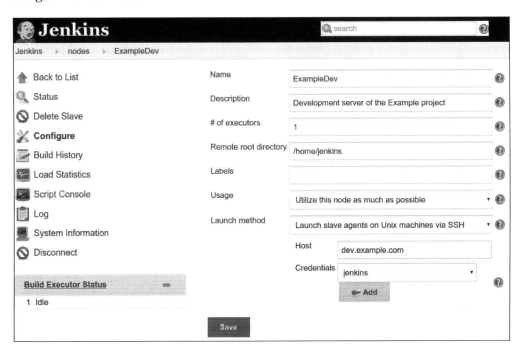

Here, we are specifying how to reach and access the server. We have set the **Host** field to `dev.example.com` and the **Credentials** field to use the default `jenkins` credentials (Go to **Manage Jenkins** | **Manage Credentials** if you need to change this). This setup will then translate to Jenkins running `ssh jenkins@dev.example.com` in order to run jobs at the development server.

Now that we added the development environment as a Jenkins node, we can create a job that uses it. Let's click on **New Item** at the Jenkins administration homepage to add the job. Name it `Sync Production to Development`, select **Freestyle Project**, and click on **Next**. In the following screenshot, we can configure our new job. Here are the form fields that we should set up: The first one defines in which server this job should run, where we will choose the `ExampleDev` node that we added in the previous step:

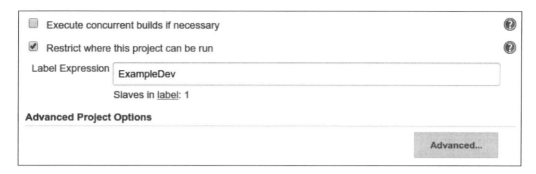

Next, at **Build Triggers**, we will make this job to run nightly at 3 AM. The following screenshot shows how we define this by typing H 3 * * *. This is a common way to define periods of time used by crontab, Jenkins, and other systems. The question icon next to the text area contains useful examples for you to define a different period of time. Furthermore, Jenkins will interpret what you type in and explain it in a sentence, as you can see at the text right below the text area:

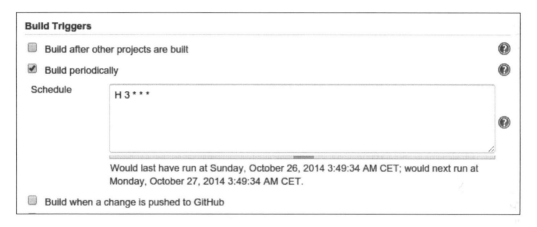

The following step is to add a **Build** step of type **Execute shell**. This will show a text area for us to type in the commands that we want Jenkins to run. We will enter the following statements to run a shell script within the scripts directory of our project, which we will implement in the next step:

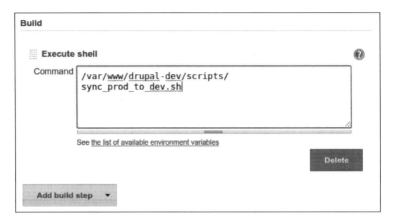

The preceding step simply runs a shell script located at the scripts/sync_prod_to_ dev.sh directory. Here are the contents of the shell script:

```
#!/usr/bin/env bash

# Jenkins script to sync database and files from Production to
Development.
cd /var/www/drupal-dev/docroot

# Sync database and files.
drush --verbose --yes sql-sync @example.prod @self
drush --verbose --yes core-rsync @example.prod:%files @self:%files
```

We could have pasted the preceding Drush commands in the Jenkins user interface, but what if the Jenkins server crashes and we lose all our jobs? By keeping shell scripts inside our project's repository, we benefit by keeping track of changes so that they evolve as the rest of the Drupal codebase does.

Read and adjust the rest of the settings for this job to suit your needs and click on **Save**. You can test it by clicking on the **Build Now** link on the left navigation menu and then inspecting the Jenkins console output.

Congratulations! You have automated a job to run periodically. Now, Jenkins will take care of keeping the development environment's database and files up to date with production.

# Fine-tuning the development database

Now that we have set up a job to periodically obtain a fresh database copy from production, it's time to add a few enhancements to it. There are a few things that the production environment's database contains, which we do not need in the development environment:

- It has personal information such as names, usernames, and passwords
- It might contain extra tables that do not need to be downloaded
- It might use modules that send e-mail notifications
- It has development and data modeling modules in disabled status

The following sections will do a few iterations on the commands which are executed by the Jenkins job in order to fine tune the database of the development environment so that the team can work with it more comfortably.

# Recreating the database on sql-sync

The `sql-sync` command has an option called `--create-db`. When used, Drush recreates the destination database prior to installing the database dump extracted from the source site (in this case, production). This option will save you more than one headache. The reason is that if you do not recreate the database, you won't be dropping tables that are not used anymore in the project. Here are a couple of scenarios where not using `--create-db` can cause trouble:

- If a field is removed in production, its data and revision tables won't be dropped from development when you run `sql-sync`. Now, if the field is added back again and exported to code through the `Features` module when you run the `updatepath` command in the development environment, you will get a SQL error saying that `Features` attempted to create a field table that already existed in your database.

- If a module was uninstalled but not all of its tables were removed, the next time you install the module, the installation process will fail because it will try to create a table that already exists.

Long story short: use this setting every time you use the `sql-sync` command. Here is what our shell script at `scripts/sync_prod_to_dev.sh` looks like after adding this setting:

```
#!/usr/bin/env bash

# Jenkins script to sync database and files from Production to
Development.
```

```
cd /var/www/drupal-dev/docroot

# Sync database and files.
drush --verbose --yes sql-sync @example.prod @self --create-db
drush --verbose --yes core-rsync @example.prod:%files @self:%files
```

# Excluding table data from production

Just as we defined in the previous chapter, a list of tables whose data was to be ignored by `sql-sync` when copying development's database into our local environment, we want to do the same when we copy the production environment's database into development. We already have the array of tables to exclude at `drush/drushrc.php` as `$options['structure-tables']['common']`. This array excludes cache tables, the search index, and other tables that contain data that we do not need to download. We can exclude the data of these tables easily by adjusting production's Drush site alias. Here is what it looks like after adjusting it at `drush/aliases/example.aliases.drushrc.php`:

```
// Production environment.
$aliases['prod'] = array(
  'root' => '/var/www/exampleprod/docroot',
  'uri' => 'http://www.example.com',
  'remote-host' => www.example.com',
  'remote-user' => 'exampleprod',
  'command-specific' => array (
    'sql-dump' => array (
      'structure-tables-key' => 'common',
    ),
  ),
);
```

That's it. Now, when Jenkins runs `sql-sync`, it will load production's site alias and therefore load the list of tables to exclude.

# Ignoring tables from production

Let's suppose now that production has a few tables that we don't want to be created in the development environment. This scenario usually happens after you have run a data migration using the `Migrate` module (`https://www.drupal.org/project/migrate`) from a legacy site to Drupal.

The `Migrate` module uses a set of custom tables to track the status of the migration process. Once it has completed, these tables will stay in the production environment. We do not need to download these tables from production to development. This is why we will use the `skip-tables` option to completely ignore them when running the `sql-sync` command. The `Migrate` module table names look like the following code:

**migrate_log**

**migrate_map_source_a**

**migrate_map_source_b**

**migrate_message_source_a**

**migrate_message_source_b**

**migrate_status**

These tables might contain a considerable amount of data depending on how much content was imported from the legacy website. We definitely do not need them in the development environment. Therefore, we will first add the `$options['skip-tables']['common']` option to our Drush configuration file in order to match these table names and then reference it at the site alias definition of the production environment. Here is our Drush configuration file at `drush/drushrc.php` after adding the list of tables to skip:

```php
<?php

/**
 * @file
 * Drush configuration for Sample project.
 */

/**
 * List of tables whose *data* is skipped by the 'sql-dump' and 'sql-sync'
 * commands when the "--structure-tables-key=common" option is
 * provided.
 */
$options['structure-tables']['common'] = array('cache', 'cache_*',
'history', 'search_*', 'sessions', 'watchdog');

/**
 * List of tables to be omitted entirely from SQL dumps made by the
 * 'sql-dump'
```

```
 * and 'sql-sync' commands when the "--skip-tables-key=common" option
is
 * provided on the command line.  This is useful if your database
contains
 * non-Drupal tables used by some other application or during a
migration for
 * example.  You may add new tables to the existing array or add a new
element.
 */
$options['skip-tables']['common'] = array('migrate_*');

// Shell aliases.
$options['shell-aliases']['syncdb'] = '--verbose --yes sql-sync @
example.dev @self --create-db';
$options['shell-aliases']['syncfiles'] = '--verbose --yes rsync @
example.dev:%files/ @self:%files/';
```

The `$options['skip-tables']['common']` setting accepts wildcards, so just with a pattern like `migrate_*`, we will exclude all the migration tables when running `sql-sync`. The last step is to reference this array at our production's site alias at `drush/aliases/example.aliases.drushrc.inc`:

```
// Production environment.
$aliases['prod'] = array(
  'root' => '/var/www/exampleprod/docroot',
  'uri' => 'http://www.example.com',
  'remote-host' => 'www.example.com',
  'remote-user' => 'exampleprod',
  'command-specific' => array (
    'sql-dump' => array (
      'structure-tables-key' => 'common',
      'skip-tables-key' => 'common',
    ),
  ),
);
```

Note that the setting is for the `sql-dump` command instead of the `sql-sync` command. The reason for this is that Drush uses `sql-dump` as a subcommand while running `sql-sync` in order to obtain a database dump. From now on, our Jenkins job will exclude migration tables in the resulting database dump to be installed in development. The `sql-sync` command will take less time to complete because the database dump to download will be smaller. As a consequence, when your team runs the Drush shell alias `syncdb`, it will download a smaller database from the development environment, thus making everyone happy.

# Sanitizing data

So, now we have a Jenkins job that downloads the production environment's database into development, excluding the data of some tables and ignoring migration tables. However, we are not doing any sanitization of compromising data. I found a very good definition of data sanitization at Wikipedia:

> *"Sanitization is the process of removing sensitive information from a document or other medium, so that it may be distributed to a broader audience."*

In our particular scenario, what we want to do is to reset usernames, passwords, personal data, and privileged data in the development database so that when the team downloads it, they get safe data to work with. Fortunately, the `sql-sync` command has a `--sanitize` option that resets all user e-mails to `user+%uid@localhost` and passwords to the literal `password;`. Additionally, it offers hook for us to add extra sanitizations.

Let's suppose that our project's users have a `Full Name` field that we also want to sanitize. We will now implement `hook_drush_sql_sync_sanitize()` at the bottom of our policy file located at `drush/commands/policy.drush.inc` with the following SQL statements, which will sanitize the field tables:

```php
<?php

/**
 * @file
 * Policy rules for Example project.
 */

// ... some other Drush hooks that we implemented before go here.

/**
 * Implements hook_drush_sql_sync_sanitize().
```

```
 *
 * Custom sql-sync sanitization to alter user's Full name. It is used
by Drush
 * when sql-sync is run with the --sanitize option.
 *
 * @see sql_drush_sql_sync_sanitize().
 */
function policy_drush_sql_sync_sanitize($source) {
  drush_sql_register_post_sync_op('policy-sanitize-full-name',
dt('Reset the full name of all users.'),
    "UPDATE field_data_field_full_name
     SET field_full_name_value = CONCAT('user+', entity_id);");
  drush_sql_register_post_sync_op('policy-sanitize-full-name-
revisions', dt('Reset the full name revisions of all users.'),
    "UPDATE field_revision_field_full_name
     SET field_full_name_value = CONCAT('user+', entity_id);");
}
```

The preceding hook resets the value of the Full Name field in the field_data_
field_full_name and field_revision_field_full_name tables to something
like user+1, 1 being the user's ID. The first table contains the actual data for each
user's full name, and the second table is used by Drupal to keep track of the different
revisions of this field (when you change a user's full name and click on **Save**, a new
revision is created). Let's now add the sanitize option to our shell script that syncs
production with development at scripts/sync_prod_to_dev.sh so that Drush will
run sanitization tasks after completing sql-sync:

```
#!/usr/bin/env bash

# Jenkins script to sync database and files from Production to
Development.
cd /var/www/drupal-dev/docroot

# Sync database and files.
drush --verbose --yes sql-sync @example.prod @self --create-db
--sanitize
drush --verbose --yes core-rsync @example.prod:%files @self:%files
```

Now, let's force the Jenkins job to run immediately by clicking on **Build Now** at the Jenkins' administration interface. Here is an excerpt of the output while `sql-sync` is running:

```
Starting to import dump file onto Destination database.          [ok]
...
Starting to sanitize target database on Destination.             [ok]
/usr/bin/php /usr/share/drush-head/drush.php --php=/usr/bin/php
--backend=2 --verbose --strict=0                                [notice]
--root=/home/juampy/projects/example/docroot --uri=http://default sql-
sanitize   --create-db --sanitize 2>&1
```

Drush's `sql-sync` command internally dispatches the `sql-sanitize` command in the destination database (in this case, the development environment) to run sanitization queries. The `sql-sanitize` command will invoke the hook that we implemented at `drush/commands/policy.drush.inc`, so our custom sanitization queries will run as well. Here is the last bit of the command's output:

```
Initialized Drupal site example.prod at sites/default          [notice]
The following post-sync operations will be done on the destination:
  * Reset the full name of all users.
  * Reset the full name revisions of all users.
  * Reset passwords and email addresses in users table
  * Truncate Drupal's sessions table
Do you really want to sanitize the current database? (y/n): y
Command dispatch complete                                       [notice]
```

Here is our confirmation: e-mails, passwords, and full names were sanitized. Additionally, the sessions table was truncated, which is not needed because we are not downloading the data of that table, but this is how the `sql-sanitize` command behaves by default. Ta-da! Now, you and your team can work safely with a database which does not have compromising data.

# Preventing e-mails from being sent

The development database is now lean and safe, thanks to the optimizations that we did in previous sections. It's now time to run some extra tasks to reconfigure the development environment's database after it has synced with production. We will start by disabling e-mail submission.

By sanitizing user e-mails as we did in the previous section, we know that our users won't get any test e-mails. However, who knows? There might be some custom code that sends an e-mail manually, which Drupal won't catch. Here are some of the options that we have to avoid this from happening:

- If we know our codebase, we can just ignore it and let e-mails be sent to dummy e-mail addresses. Not my preference, but still an option.

- There are a few modules in Drupal.org to alter e-mail submission such as Reroute Email (https://www.drupal.org/project/reroute_email), which redirects e-mails to a given address or Devel (https://www.drupal.org/project/devel), which writes them to a file.

- You can also reroute all e-mail being sent to be written to a log at the server level by following the instructions at this article from the Lullabot blog: https://www.lullabot.com/blog/article/oh-no-my-laptop-just-sent-notifications-10000-users.

If e-mail is important for your project, then you might want to log it to a file so that it can be debugged. If it is not, then redirecting it to a dummy account such as dummy@example.com should be enough. For our example project, we will go for the simplest solution, which consists of installing Reroute Email (http://drupal.org/project/reroute_email) and redirecting all mail to dummy@example.com.

Here is our Jenkins script to sync production with development after we add a few commands to reroute e-mail submission at scripts/sync_prod_to_dev.sh:

```bash
#!/usr/bin/env bash

# Jenkins script to sync database and files from Production to
Development.
cd /var/www/drupal-dev/docroot

# Sync database and files.
drush --verbose --yes sql-sync @example.prod @self --create-db
--sanitize
drush --verbose --yes core-rsync @example.prod:%files @self:%files

# Disable email submission.
drush --verbose --yes pm-enable reroute_email
drush --verbose --yes variable-set reroute_email_enable 1
drush --verbose --yes variable-set reroute_email_address 'dummy@
example.com'
drush --verbose --yes variable-set reroute_email_enable_message 1
```

In the preceding script, we installed the `Reroute Email` module and then set a few variables that the module uses:

- `reroute_email_enable`: This is a flag to activate e-mail rerouting
- `reroute_email_address`: This is the address designated to receive e-mails
- `reroute_email_enable_message`: This is a flag that, when active, adds a piece of text to the body informing that the e-mail was rerouted and where it should have been sent instead

E-mail submission won't be a problem anymore in our development environment and in the local environments of our team. Here is a chance for you to take a look at the project where you are currently working. Log in to your production environment and run `drush pm-list --status=enabled`. Inspect this list and ask yourself, do you need to disable any of those modules in development? Do you need to tweak any of their settings? If you do, then simply add your commands at the bottom of `scripts/sync_prod_to_dev.sh`.

The `settings.php` file is also a good place to overwrite configuration variables as per environment. If you have specific `settings.php` files for each environment or a way to identify the current environment at `settings.php` (for example, Acquia environments have a variable called `$_ENV['AH_SITE_ENVIRONMENT']`), then you can overwrite the configuration variables there.

# Running post sql-sync tasks in local environments

We have come a long way to here. So far, we built together a workflow from production to development and provided the team with two simple commands:

- `syncdb`: This is a command to download a copy of the development environment's database
- `syncfiles`: This is a command to download files from the `files` directory into the development environment

This is the same as when we added extra tasks after syncing production to development; we would like to automatically adjust the database configuration of a local environment once `sql-sync` completes. Here are some of the things we will do:

- Enable user interface modules that are disabled in production and development, such as `Views UI` and `Field UI`
- Enable development modules such as `Devel`, `Database Logging`, and `Stage File Proxy`

- Disable production modules such as Update, Purge, or Memcache
- Adjust environment variables to fine tune installed modules and disable caches

The preceding list is what I consider the most common list of things that a developer would need. Depending on your background and the nature of the project, you might like to adjust it even further and add new items.

There are several ways to implement the requirements of the preceding list. Here are some of the alternatives:

- We could write a custom command and append it to the Drush shell alias syncdb so that it runs automatically
- We could implement drush_hook_post_sql_sync() in a command file and run Drush statements when the source alias is @dev.example.com and the target alias is @self
- We could install the Rebuild project (https://www.drupal.org/project/rebuild) and define the preceding list in a YAML file for the command to process it
- We could use the devify command, which ships with Drupal Boilerplate and is available for us at drush/commands

In our case, we will use the devify command due to its simplicity. Drupal Boilerplate now hosts our example project so that the devify command can be found at drush/commands/build.drush.inc. Let's jump to the command line and inspect its documentation:

```
$ cd /home/juampy/projects/example/docroot
$ drush help devify
Configures the current database for development.
Examples:
 drush devify              Uses command default values to set up a
                           database for development.


 drush devify --enable-modules=xhprof,devel      Enables XHProf and Devel
                                                 modules


 drush devify --reset-variables=site_mail=local@local.com,file_temporary_
path=/tmp
```

```
Resets site_mail and file_temporary_path variables.


Options:
 --delete-variables                              A comma separated list of
                                                 variables to delete.
 --reset-variables                               A comma separated list of
                                                 variables to reset with the
                                                 format foo=var,hey=ho.
 --disable-modules                               A comma separated list of
                                                 modules to disable.
 --enable-modules                                A comma separated list of
                                                 modules to enable.
```

As we can see from the preceding output, the command accepts a list of variables to delete, a list of variables to reset, a list of modules to enable, and a list of modules to disable. Our command invocation would be very long in order to make all the adjustments that we mentioned at the start of this section; so, we will instead define these options at our Drush configuration file at `drush/drushrc.php`. Here is the bottom of the file after we add the list of options for the `devify` command to use:

```php
<?php

/**
 * @file
 * Drush configuration for Sample project.
 */

/**
 * List of tables whose *data* is skipped by the 'sql-dump' and 'sql-
sync'
 * commands when the "--structure-tables-key=common" option is
provided.
 */
$options['structure-tables']['common'] = array('cache', 'cache_*',
'history', 'search_*', 'sessions', 'watchdog');

/**
```

```
 * List of tables to be omitted entirely from SQL dumps made by the
'sql-dump'
 * and 'sql-sync' commands when the "--skip-tables-key=common" option
is
 * provided on the command line.  This is useful if your database
contains
 * non-Drupal tables used by some other application or during a
migration for
 * example.  You may add new tables to the existing array or add a new
element.
 */
$options['skip-tables']['common'] = array('migrate_*');

// Shell aliases.
$options['shell-aliases']['syncdb'] = '!drush --verbose --yes sql-sync
@example.dev @self --create-db && drush devify';
$options['shell-aliases']['syncfiles'] = '--verbose --yes rsync @
example.dev:%files/ @self:%files/';

/**
 * Command options for devify command.
 * @see build.drush.inc
 */
$command_specific['devify'] = array(
  'enable-modules' => array(
    'dblog',
    'devel',
    'field_ui',
    'reroute_email',
    'stage_file_proxy',
    'views_ui',
  ),
  'disable-modules' => array(
    'update',
    'purge',
  ),
  'reset-variables' => array(
    // File management settings.
```

```
    'file_temporary_path' => '/tmp/',
    // Cache settings.
    'cache' => FALSE,
    'block_cache' => FALSE,
    'preprocess_css' => FALSE,
    'preprocess_js' => FALSE,
    // Stage file proxy settings.
    'stage_file_proxy_origin' => 'http://dev.example.com',
    'stage_file_proxy_origin_dir' => 'sites/default/files',
    'stage_file_proxy_hotlink' => TRUE,
  ),
  );
```

The above array of settings name $command_specific['devify'] will be used by the devify command when we run it. It will enable the given list of modules, disable a couple of ones, and reset some variables.

Within the list of modules to enable, there is a Stage File Proxy module (https://www.drupal.org/project/stage_file_proxy). I found this module extremely helpful while working locally on large projects with a huge amount of media files at the files directory. The module uses what it calls a *proxy origin* to fetch files from it when Drupal can't find a file at your local files directory. This frees you from having to download files from the development environment to your local environment in order to obtain, for example, images from the latest content in the website. It is a great tool because it saves you both time and hard disk space.

The Stage File Proxy module needs a few variables to be defined after being installed for it to work. Here, they are along with the values we have given to them:

- 'stage_file_proxy_origin' => 'http://dev.example.com': This is the source to fetch images from. We are using the development environment as the proxy because its files are in sync with our local database.

- 'stage_file_proxy_origin_dir' => 'sites/default/files': This is the directory where files are served in the development environment.

- 'stage_file_proxy_hotlink' => TRUE: This setting tells Stage File Proxy not to download files to our local environment, but instead serve them directly from the development environment through a 301 response code. This will make pages in your local environment to load faster.

We have also altered the Drush shell alias `syncdb`, which now looks like the following code:

```
// Shell aliases.
$options['shell-aliases']['syncdb'] = '!drush --verbose --yes sql-sync
@example.dev @self --create-db && drush devify';
$options['shell-aliases']['syncfiles'] = '--verbose --yes rsync @
example.dev:%files/ @self:%files/';
```

The shell alias now starts with `!drush`. This tells Drush not to prepend `drush` when running the shell alias, which gives us the chance to append additional commands with `&&`. Now our team, after running `drush syncdb`, will not only get a lean and safe database to work with, but also will have everything they need to work comfortably. If any customizations have to be made, they can enter them at their `settings.php` file or even define their own Drush shell aliases at `$HOME/.drush/drushrc.php`.

# Summary

First of all, thanks! I am so glad that you made it up to this point. This chapter was a hands-on training in defining a development workflow. We used a good amount of what is available in Drush core: configuration, shell aliases, commands, and site aliases. Each feature served as a piece of the final puzzle.

We started the chapter by moving our example Drupal project into Drupal Boilerplate, a default directory structure for Drupal projects. We moved all our custom Drush code (configuration, commands, and site aliases) out of Drupal and then added a small piece of code for Drush to discover the new location.

We created a Jenkins job to periodically copy the database and files from the production environment into the development environment. Then, we optimized this process as much as possible by reducing the amount of data that gets downloaded, sanitizing compromising data, and rerouting email submission.

We closed the chapter by offering a way to automate extra tasks to run in local environments after obtaining a copy of the development environment's database. Things such as enabling development modules and disabling caches can be accomplished easily with the `devify` command.

Thank you again for reading this book. I hope that you enjoyed reading it as much as I did writing it. My head is empty now. This was all I could share with you to help you master Drupal development with Drush. See you in the issue queues!

# Index

requisites, verifying 106
site aliases, using in commands 110, 111
**remote server**
accessing, through public key 106, 107
**Reroute Email module**
reroute_email_address 153
reroute_email_enable flag 153
reroute_email_enable_message flag 153
URL 152
**rollback mechanism 85**
**RSS feed**
URL 53

# S

**sample Drush command, Batch API**
about 58, 59
output, verifying 61, 62
running 61, 62
**sanitization 149**
**scripts**
running 63
**scripts, for nodes creation 66, 67**
**scripts, for revisions creation 66, 67**
**Secure Shell**
URL, for wiki 106
**single command**
update path, turning into 86-90
**site alias**
about 104
moving, out of Drupal 132, 133
update path, running with 119, 120
using, in commands 110, 111
**site alias, of group**
command, running on 112
**site alias support**
adding, to update path 114
**source code**
viewing, of function 99, 100
**special site aliases**
about 112
command, running on all site aliases
of group 112
current project, referencing with @self
alias 113, 114
Drupal bootstrap, avoiding with @none
alias 113

**sql-sync command**
about 127, 145
development database, recreating on 145
tables, ignoring on 127-129
**SSH**
URL 49
**Stage File Proxy module**
URL 157
variables, with values 157
**standard streams**
STDERR 70
STDIN 70
STDOUT 70
URL 70
**streams**
references 71
**strict-option-handling command 81**
**Strongarm module**
URL 46
**syncdb command 153**
**syncfiles command 153**

# T

**tables**
ignoring, on sql-sync command 127-129
**task**
on demand 43
one-off 43
periodic 43
running, outside cron 52
URL, for Wikipedia definition 43
**team**
development database, configuring for 140
Drush shell aliases, defining for 122-124
**trap, for breaking Drupal's registry**
preparing 24, 25

# U

**Ubuntu**
URL 9
**update path**
about 22, 23
results, analyzing 37, 38
running, on different environment 36, 37
running, with site alias 119, 120

## Thank you for buying
## Drush for Developers
### *Second Edition*

# About Packt Publishing

Packt, pronounced 'packed', published its first book, *Mastering phpMyAdmin for Effective MySQL Management*, in April 2004, and subsequently continued to specialize in publishing highly focused books on specific technologies and solutions.

Our books and publications share the experiences of your fellow IT professionals in adapting and customizing today's systems, applications, and frameworks. Our solution-based books give you the knowledge and power to customize the software and technologies you're using to get the job done. Packt books are more specific and less general than the IT books you have seen in the past. Our unique business model allows us to bring you more focused information, giving you more of what you need to know, and less of what you don't.

Packt is a modern yet unique publishing company that focuses on producing quality, cutting-edge books for communities of developers, administrators, and newbies alike. For more information, please visit our website at www.packtpub.com.

# About Packt Open Source

In 2010, Packt launched two new brands, Packt Open Source and Packt Enterprise, in order to continue its focus on specialization. This book is part of the Packt Open Source brand, home to books published on software built around open source licenses, and offering information to anybody from advanced developers to budding web designers. The Open Source brand also runs Packt's Open Source Royalty Scheme, by which Packt gives a royalty to each open source project about whose software a book is sold.

# Writing for Packt

We welcome all inquiries from people who are interested in authoring. Book proposals should be sent to author@packtpub.com. If your book idea is still at an early stage and you would like to discuss it first before writing a formal book proposal, then please contact us; one of our commissioning editors will get in touch with you.

We're not just looking for published authors; if you have strong technical skills but no writing experience, our experienced editors can help you develop a writing career, or simply get some additional reward for your expertise.

## Drush User's Guide

ISBN: 978-1-84951-798-0 Paperback: 140 pages

A practical guide to Drush, Drupal's command line interface, helping you work with your Drupal sites more effectively

1. Stop clicking around administration pages and start issuing commands straight to your Drupal sites.

2. Write your own commands, hook in to alter existing ones, and extend the toolkit with a long list of contributed modules.

3. A practical guide full of examples and step-by-step instructions to start using Drush right from chapter 1.

## Drupal 7 Development by Example Beginner's Guide

ISBN: 978-1-84951-680-8 Paperback: 366 pages

Follow the creation of a Drupal website to learn, by example, the key concepts of Drupal 7 development and HTML5

1. A hands-on, example-driven guide to programming Drupal websites.

2. Discover a number of new features for Drupal 7 through practical and interesting examples while building a fully functional recipe sharing website.

3. Learn about web content management, multimedia integration, and e-commerce in Drupal 7.

Please check **www.PacktPub.com** for information on our titles

## Drupal 7 Cookbook

ISBN: 978-1-84951-796-6          Paperback: 324 pages

Over 70 recipes that will advance your Drupal skills from novice to pro

1. Install, set up, and manage a Drupal site, and discover how to get the most out of creating and displaying content.

2. Become familiar with creating new content types and use them to create and publish content using views, blocks, and panels.

3. Learn how to work with images, documents, and videos and how to integrate them with Facebook, Twitter, and AddThis.

## Building E-commerce Sites with Drupal Commerce Cookbook

ISBN: 978-1-78216-122-6          Paperback: 206 pages

Over 50 recipes to help you build engaging, responsive E-commerce sites with Drupal Commerce

1. Learn how to build attractive e-commerce sites with Drupal Commerce.

2. Customize your Drupal Commerce store for maximum impact.

3. Reviewed by the creators of Drupal Commerce – The Commerce Guys.

Please check **www.PacktPub.com** for information on our titles

Made in the USA
Middletown, DE
13 October 2015